FLOWERS THAT LAST FOREVER

BY THE SAME AUTHOR

Growing Herbs for the Kitchen, Gray's Publishing, Ltd., Sidney, B.C., Canada

Profitable Herb Growing at Home, Garden Way Publishing, Pownal, Vermont

Growing Herbs and Plants for Dyeing, distributed by The Unicorn, Books for Craftsmen, Inc., Petaluma, California

Growing and Using Herbs Successfully, Garden Way Publishing, Pownal, Vermont

FLOWERS
THAT LAST FOREVER

GROWING, HARVESTING, AND PRESERVING

BETTY E. M. JACOBS

Illustrations by
Kay Gough and Judy Eliason

A GARDEN WAY PUBLISHING BOOK

STOREY COMMUNICATIONS, INC.
POWNAL, VERMONT

🐦 🐦 🐦

The information in this book is true and complete to the best of our knowledge. All recommendations are made without guarantee on the part of the author or Storey Communications, Inc. The author and publisher disclaim all liability incurred with the use of this information.

🐦 🐦 🐦

Text and cover designed and produced by Cindy McFarland
Cover (front and back) photograph by Richard Brown
Typesetting by Accura Type & Design, Inc.

Printed in the United States by The Alpine Press

First printing, October 1988

The name Garden Way Publishing has been licensed to Storey Communications, Inc., by Garden Way, Inc.

Library of Congress Cataloging-in-Publication Data

Jacobs, Betty E. M.
  Flowers that last forever.

  "A Garden Way Publishing book."
  Bibliography: p.
  Includes index.
  1. Everlasting flowers. 2. Ornamental grasses. 3. Plants—Collection and preservation.
4. Dried flower arrangement. I. Title.
SB428.5.J33   1988   635.9'73   87-46445
ISBN 0-88266-540-5
ISBN 0-88266-516-2 (pbk.)

CONTENTS

In memory of
two people who loved their gardens—
my mother, Eleanor Brecknell,
and
my mother-in-law, Marjorie Jacobs.

ACKNOWLEDGMENTS

I am indebted to so many people for their help.

I should particularly like to thank the staff of the Victoria Public Libraries and the Vancouver Island Regional Libraries who, without exception, were always willing to help me in so many ways.

My thanks to Ellen at Munro's Book Store in Victoria. To Marion who told me all about making greeting cards; to Deborah for showing me how she made her exquisite pressed pictures; to Moira who makes such beautiful bookmarks; to Adrienne who revealed some of the secrets of commercial growing; to Lena who showed me her basement full of dried flowers for her classes; and to Rosemary, always so willing to discuss knotty problems and to give me the benefit of her horticultural knowledge.

Also to Jack and his "ham" radio friend in Cordoba, Argentina, who kept me in close touch with my artist, Kay Gough, while she was working so hard on many of the illustrations in this book.

To all the people at Garden Way Publishing/Storey Communications who made this book possible.

To Paula for never failing to come when she was needed. And finally to my husband who not only put up with the disruption of his routine over many, many months, but also sorted out and typed the final manuscript. Indeed without his help there would have been no *Flowers That Last Forever*.

If you have two loaves of bread
sell one and buy a flower.

PREFACE

SOME YEARS AGO, when my husband and I still had our herb farm on Vancouver Island, we grew a lot of everlasting flowers and plants. Recently there has been renewed interest in these lovely and useful plants. I felt that a combination of my experiences during those years and the information I had gathered in my gardening diaries could be made into a practical and informative book.

Because few of the Everlastings are familiar garden flowers, I have described thirty-one of them in detail, as well as how to grow, harvest, and dry them, in Part I of this book. The thirty-one plants described include the True Everlastings, with their naturally papery petals or seedpods, and the Perpetuelles (easily dried by hanging and long lasting), many of which can also be called everlasting. I have also described six attractive ornamental grasses.

If you never grow anything else, these thirty-one plants will give you an excellent variety of dried material to work with. All of them can be preserved with a minimum of trouble, and when dried will retain good color and form. You will have access to flowers at all seasons of the year, even if you live in a climate where winters are severe and fresh flowers expensive, or in a hot climate where summer flowers are hard to come by. You can make arrangements ahead of time for special occasions, and if you keep them airtight under glass they could actually last forever. Dried flowers are economical and versatile: without need of water, they can be used in ways that wouldn't be possible with fresh flowers.

Part II of the book describes a number of ways to dry and preserve the flowers and leaves of plants that are not "natural" driers. Many of these plants are familiar garden inhabitants, others can be purchased from the florist, and some can be found in the wild.

In Part III you will discover *what* you can do with the dried-plant material, *how* to do it, and how to store it when it is not in use.

So let me wish you every success in growing, drying, and using your dried-plant material. Be sure to keep a record of all your trials and errors—it will be invaluable to you as the years go by.

PART I

SPECIES DESCRIPTIONS OF THIRTY-ONE EVERLASTING PLANTS

Illustrations by Kay Gough

LIST OF
THE THIRTY-ONE EVERLASTING PLANTS
*LATIN NAME/*COMMON NAME

LATIN NAME	COMMON NAME
Achillea filipendulina	Yarrow, fern-leaf
Amaranthus caudatus	Love-lies-bleeding
Ammobium alatum	Everlasting sand flower
Anaphalis margaritacea	Pearly everlasting
Briza maxima	Pearl grass
Calluna vulgaris	Heather
Carlina acaulis	Carline thistle
Carthamus tinctorius	Safflower
Catananche caerulea	Cupid's-dart
Celosia cristata	Cockscomb
Coix lacryma-jobi	Job's-tears
Cortaderia selloana	Pampas grass
Cynara cardunculus	Cardoon
Dipsacus sativus	Teasel
Echinops ritro	Globe thistle, small
Eryngium & species	Eryngo
Gomphrena globosa	Globe amaranth
Gypsophila paniculata	Baby's-breath
Helichrysum bracteatum	Strawflower
Helipterum roseum	Acroclinium
Hordeum jubatum	Squirreltail grass
Lagurus ovatus	Hare's-tail grass
Limonium sinuatum	Statice
Lonas annua	African daisy
Lunaria annua	Honesty
Moluccella laevis	Bells-of-Ireland
Physalis alkekengi	Chinese-lantern plant
Psylliostachys suworowii	Pink pokers
Scabiosa stellata	Starflower
Stipa pennata	Feather grass, European
Xeranthemum annuum	Immortelle

FIRST!
READ THIS INTRODUCTION

THROUGHOUT THE BOOK you will find plants identified by
their Latin/botanical names as well as their common ones. The
reason for this is to avoid confusion. Plants often have several common
names, and conversely the *same* common name is often used to identify different plants.

For instance, soapwort (*Saponaria officinalis*) is also called bounc-
ing bet, which is also one of the names for wild pansies (*Viola tricolor*).
Just to confuse you, these wild pansies are also called love-lies-
bleeding; but that is the common name of *Amaranthus caudatus* too!
That's not too complicated. But one of the many fascinating names
of the pitcher plant (*Sarracenia purpurea*) is fly trap, which is also a
common name for bitter root (*Apocynum androsaemifolium*). But bitter
root is also called milkweed and many of the *Asclepias* species are also
known by that name. Now do you see why Latin names are necessary for foolproof identification?

Detailed information about the thirty-one everlasting plants in
Part I is found under each one's *most-used* common name; they are
arranged alphabetically by that common name in Part I. You will find
a Latin/Common name list of these same plants on the opposite page.
In addition, the index at the back of the book lists every Latin and
common name found on the pages herein.

So whichever name you know your plant by, you should be able
to find the information you need with no trouble at all. I should mention that sometimes the first part of the Latin name is also used as
a common name. Yarrow, for example, is often listed as achillea,
cupid's-dart as catanche, and so on. Thus, if you can't find the plant
you are looking for under its common name, look for it under its Latin
name in the plant index.

For each plant the information you need to grow, harvest, and dry is listed under the following headings.

LATIN NAME	Usually in two parts: *Helichrysum bracteatum*. *Helichrysum* is the **genus**, *bracteatum* the **species**. All Latin names herein follow the nomenclature established in *Hortus Third*, which has been compiled by the Liberty Hyde Bailey Hortorium of Cornell University and published by Macmillan.
FAMILY	Or **natural order** (n.o.). You will notice a likeness in the appearance of plants of the same botanical family. For example, the African daisy, acroclinium, and globe thistle all belong to the Compositae family, as do lettuce, dandelion, and chicory.
& KNOWN AS	The same plant may be known by more than one **common name**. If it is, they will be listed here. Sometimes the same common name is used for two or more different plants as was explained earlier. This is why it is important to identify plants by their Latin names. So when ordering seed or buying plants be sure the supplier gives the Latin name in addition to the common ones, which may be folk names, popular names, or names often found in seed catalogs, but not necessarily those used by botanists.
LIFE SPAN	A **hardy annual** (h.a.) is a plant raised from seed, which flowers and dies within the year.
	A **half-hardy annual** (h.h.a.) cannot stand frost, and is usually started indoors. It is not planted out until all danger of frost is past. It will usually die with the first fall frost.
	A **biennial** (b) is sown one year, and produces flowers and seed the following year before it dies. Sometimes the life span of a biennial may be prolonged by removing flower heads as they form.
	A **hardy perennial** (h.p.) lives for at least two years and sometimes for as long as twenty. Some stay green all winter, others die back and reappear in spring.
HABITAT	The natural and/or original home of the plant.
APPEARANCE	A brief description of the plant, whether the blooms are single petaled or double (multiple), when they bloom, and the color of the flowers. The botanical drawings that appear opposite each of the thirty-one plant entries make a long description unnecessary.

SOIL	The type of soil best suited to the plant, and whether or not good drainage is necessary.
LOCATION	Whether the plant thrives in sun, shade, or partial shade, and if it needs shelter from the wind.
PROPAGATION & CARE BY SEED	When to sow the seed and at what depth. The optimum air temperature for good germination. How long the seed will take to germinate. The care of the seedlings: whether to thin them out or to transplant them, what distance apart to plant seedlings, and any other cultural requirements, such as pruning or pinching back of the plants.
VEGETATIVE	Most perennial plants can be propagated vegetatively as well as by seed. Recommendations as to what type of vegetative propagation to use (division, root cuttings, stem cuttings), how much space the plants need in the garden, and any other special cultural requirements of that particular plant.
HARVESTING & DRYING	When to harvest the flowers and grasses to ensure that they retain their form and color when dry. How to prepare them for drying. The preferred method or methods for drying plants is given here (the contents gives method numbers within each broad drying/preserving section).
NOTE	Special information about the plant, such as details of other varieties, their place in the garden, their suitability as cut flowers, etc.

ACROCLINIUM
Helipterum roseum

ACROCLINIUM

LATIN NAME	*Helipterum roseum*
FAMILY	Compositae
& KNOWN AS	Australian everlasting and immortelle flower (these two names are used for several other everlasting flowers). Also called Sunray.
LIFE SPAN	Half-hardy annual
HABITAT	Western Australia
APPEARANCE	Grows to a height of about 18 inches (45 cm). The stems are stiff and upright, the gray-green leaves narrow and the flowers daisylike. Though originally rose colored and single white, yellow and various shades of pink in both single and double forms are now obtainable. The seeds are usually sold as a mixture, often under the name of *Acroclinium grandiflorum*, though this name is not botanically correct. They bloom from June to September.
SOIL	A well-drained soil, rich in humus, but slightly acid. These plants will not tolerate soil that has been limed.
LOCATION	Full sun and shelter from wind.
PROPAGATION & CARE BY SEED	Sow the seed in late March or early April, 1/8 inch (3 mm) deep, where the temperature can be maintained between 55° and 65° F (13° and 18° C). In many climates this will mean an indoor sowing and later transplanting. At this temperature they should germinate in about ten to twelve days. Where springs are warm, sow outdoors in late April and do not transplant. Thin to 8 inches (20 cm) apart. Plants raised indoors should be planted out 8 inches (20 cm) apart at the same time you would plant out tomatoes; that is, after *all* danger of frost is past. Don't forget to harden them off for a week or ten days before they go out, and pinch them back if they are at all "leggy." Plants should flower about six to eight weeks after the seed is sown.
HARVESTING	Harvest just as the flowers start to open. If left until they are overmature the yellow centers will blacken. Harvest even if it means picking in wet weather, for when the

weather is wet the petals will close, but will open again as they dry, unlike most everlasting flowers.

DRYING Strip off the leaves and tie in bunches of no more than ten flowers. Hang in a dark, dry, well-ventilated place (Method 1).

NOTE Rhodanthe is a close relative of acroclinium. The species *Helipterum humboldtianum* (also known as *H. sandfordii*) has yellow flowers and is grown in exactly the same way as acroclinium, but the best way to harvest is to cut the stems as long as possible, when some of the flowers are open and some still in bud.

Acroclinium is not a particularly attractive plant for a flower border. Grow it in a row in the vegetable garden or cut-flower garden.

AFRICAN DAISY
Lonas annua

AFRICAN DAISY

LATIN NAME	*Lonas annua*
FAMILY	Compositae
& KNOWN AS	Golden ageratum, yellow ageratum
LIFE SPAN	Hardy annual, though in climates where the spring is short and cold, treat them as half-hardy annuals.
HABITAT	Mediterranean region
APPEARANCE	Grows about 12 inches (30 cm) high. The stems are firm, reddish, and branching; the leaves are downy, long, and deeply cut; and the flowers are bright yellow and grow in clusters. Blooms from July to fall; remains undamaged by light frost.
SOIL	Grow in almost any soil, as long as the drainage is good.
LOCATION	Plant in full sun.
PROPAGATION & CARE BY SEED	Sow seed outside in April, where the plants will remain. Seedlings from seed planted directly in the garden should not be transplanted, but thinned out, leaving about 12 inches (30 cm) between plants. In climates with late or cold springs, sow the seed indoors in March or early April, 1/8 inch (3 mm) deep, keeping them at a temperature of about 55° F (13° C). Seedlings grown indoors should be planted out 12 inches (30 cm) apart, after all danger of frost has passed, at the same time you plant out your tomatoes.
HARVESTING	Cut the flowers, with as long a stem as possible, just before they are fully open and before the little heads are starting to show signs of setting seed.
DRYING	Strip off the leaves, tie in bunches of four or five heads. Hang in a dark, dry, well-ventilated place, Method 1. They will also retain their color well if dried by Methods 4, 11, 12, or 14.
NOTE	African daisies are excellent in a mixed-flower border because they have such a long blooming period.

BABY'S-BREATH

LATIN NAME	*Gypsophila paniculata*
FAMILY	Caryophyllaceae
& KNOWN AS	Chalk plant
LIFE SPAN	Hardy perennial
HABITAT	Mediterranean region
APPEARANCE	Attains a height of 36 to 48 inches (90 cm to 1.20 m). Stems are wiry and branching; leaves are insignificant; and the white flowers are numerous, minute, and usually single. It blooms from midsummer until early fall. The flowers of the variety 'Bristol Fairy' are large and double.
SOIL	A deeply dug, well-limed soil is essential, with good drainage. Its roots go down very deep.
LOCATION	Plant in a dry, sunny spot.
PROPAGATION & CARE	
BY SEED	Sow the seed in the spring (about the same time as you sow beets), barely covering it, in a warm, sheltered seedbed. The resultant seedlings should be planted out 36 inches (90 cm) apart, in their permanent location, when they are about 2 inches (5 cm) high. They are unlikely to flower the first year.
VEGETATIVE	Though this species of *Gypsophila* is a perennial, it is not advisable to dig and divide the roots because they do not like to be disturbed. Cuttings may be rooted in sand, as soon as material is available in late spring or early summer. If you are fortunate enough to find a plant of the double variety ('Bristol Fairy'), and you wish to propagate it yourself, here are the directions given to me many years ago by a staff member of an English gardening magazine:

Softwood cuttings of this plant (*Gypsophila* 'Bristol Fairy') that are 2 or 3 inches (5 or 7.5 cm) long, will root readily in a cold frame in summer. Propagation can also be carried out by wedge-grafting onto root pieces of *G. paniculata*, which can be readily raised from seed. Sown in March, the roots of *G. paniculata* will be ready for grafting the following February, when they should be cut into pieces about 3 inches (7.5 cm) long. Meanwhile, stock

BABY'S-BREATH
Gypsophila paniculata

plants of G. p. 'Bristol Fairy' should be brought from the garden to a warm greenhouse so that growth will start. When the young shoots are 3 to 4 inches (7.5 to 10 cm) long they can be used as scions. The bottom of each of these shoots is trimmed to an inch-long (2.5 cm) wedge, which is then fitted into a slit made in the end of the G. p. root, the two then being tied together with raffia. The grafted roots are then placed in a closed cold frame until union is complete.

HARVESTING | Whenever there are flowers past the green bud stage, but which have not fully opened, cut the plant back, leaving 12 inches (30 cm) of stem to allow for a second cutting. In October, or before the first frost, cut the whole plant right back, close to the ground.

DRYING | Bunch it without crushing the delicate flowers. Hang upside down to dry (Method 1); or let stand in a little water that is allowed to evaporate, then dry the plant material (Method 3). To keep stems pliable, preserve baby's-breath in glycerine (Method 15).

WARNING | The *dried* stems are very brittle. Before using them in a winter arrangement, take them from their dry-storage place into a humid atmosphere and leave them for several hours. This will make stems pliable and less likely to snap.

NOTE | There is an annual baby's-breath species (*Gypsophila elegans*) that is excellent as a fresh-cut flower, but goes gray when dried. Any perennial baby's-breath can also be used fresh.

BELLS-OF-IRELAND
Moluccella laevis

BELLS-OF-IRELAND

LATIN NAME	*Moluccella laevis*
FAMILY	Labiatae
& KNOWN AS	Shellflower, old-maid's nightcap, molucca balm
LIFE SPAN	Half-hardy annual
HABITAT	Mediterranean region, Asia Minor, Syria, and Iraq
APPEARANCE	Grows to a height of 18 inches (45 cm). Stems are upright. The ornamental spikes consist of tiny white flowers surrounded by a large, green, shell-like calyx.
SOIL	Prefers a well-drained soil that is light but rich.
LOCATION	Plant in full sun.
PROPAGATION & CARE By Seed	Sow the seed in early spring, barely covering it, where a temperature of 75° F (24° C) can be maintained. At this temperature, seeds will germinate in ten to twenty days; at a lower temperature germination is erratic. When the seedlings have two true leaves, pot them into 3-inch pots. They should not be planted out in the garden until *after* the last frost date for your zone. Harden them off first, then plant them 12 inches (30 cm) apart.
HARVESTING	Cut the stems after the leaves have fallen, which will be in late summer or early fall.
DRYING	Stand the stems in a tall container, in 2 inches (5 cm) of water. When the water has evaporated, hang each stem upside down individually in a dark, dry, well-ventilated place (Method 3). The flowers can also be preserved in glycerine (Method 15). Do not hurry the drying process with warmth or plants may disintegrate.
NOTE	Bells-of-Ireland are very attractive fresh-cut flowers.

CARDOON
Cynara cardunculus

CARDOON

LATIN NAME	*Cynara cardunculus*
FAMILY	Compositae
LIFE SPAN	Hardy perennial, but needs renewal every four years
HABITAT	Southern Europe
APPEARANCE	Growing to a height of 72 inches (1.80 m), this close relative of the globe artichoke (*C. scolymus*) has large, deeply serrated, silver-gray foliage. Its stems are thick and sturdy. The purple flower heads appear in the second summer of growth, and develop into fluffy gold and bronze seedheads, which are often as much as 6 inches (15 cm) in diameter.
SOIL	Rich, well-cultivated soil is needed because cardoons are gross feeders. Prepare the soil in the fall by digging a trench 12 inches (30 cm) deep, then fork in 6 inches (15 cm) of well-rotted manure. In April (or early spring) top the manure with 4 inches (10 cm) of compost, and level with soil removed when the trench was made in the fall.
LOCATION	Full sun, but sheltered from wind.
PROPAGATION & CARE BY SEED	In late spring, sow the seed 1 inch (2.5 cm) deep, in groups of three or four seeds at intervals of 18 inches (45 cm). At a temperature of 60° F (15° C), germination will take from two to three weeks. When the seedlings are 4 inches (10 cm) high, thin them one to every 18 inches (45 cm). Drive a 72-inch (1.80 m) stake into the ground beside each seedling. When the seedlings are 12 inches (30 cm) high, tie them securely to the stakes and continue to do so as they grow. Young seedlings will transplant successfully, but mature plants do not.
NOTE	Cardoons may also be grown as a vegetable. To make the stems fit to eat, it will be necessary to blanch them. In September tie straw or corrugated brown paper around the stems. In eight weeks the stems will be ready to use.
HARVESTING	Harvest the seed heads when they are fully ripe in the fall.
DRYING	Hang them upside down in the sun, or if the weather is damp, use Methods 1, 5, 6, 7, 8, or 9.

CARLINE THISTLE
Carlina acaulis

CARLINE THISTLE

LATIN NAME	*Carlina acaulis*
FAMILY	Compositae
& KNOWN AS	Carlina, stemless carline, silver thistle
LIFE SPAN	Hardy perennial
HABITAT	The Mediterranean region of Europe
APPEARANCE	Grows 8 to 12 inches (20 to 30 cm) high; forms a rosette of stemless spiny leaves. The short-stemmed flowers bloom in early summer, and huge bronze, gold, and white flower heads are surrounded by spreading silvery white bracts. In damp weather the flowers close.
SOIL	Will grow in almost any garden soil, but good drainage is essential.
LOCATION	Plant in full sun, ideally on a rocky slope.
PROPAGATION & CARE BY SEED	Sow the seed 1/8 inch (3 mm) deep in spring, where a temperature of 65 °F (18 °C) can be maintained; they may take as long as three months to germinate. When the seedlings are about 2 inches (5 cm) high, they should be hardened off, and planted out 12 to 15 inches (30 to 45 cm) apart. Mature plants should only be transplanted when dormant, preferably in early spring before growth has started.
VEGETATIVE	Divide plants that are three or more years old in early spring.
HARVESTING	The ideal time to harvest the seed heads is when they are fully ripe.
DRYING	If, because of wet weather, it is necessary to cut them sooner, dry them in a well-ventilated room by laying them on sheets of newspaper in the sun. Or use Methods 5, 6, 7, 8, 9, or 10.

CHINESE LANTERN PLANT
Physalis alkekengi

CHINESE-LANTERN PLANT

LATIN NAME	*Physalis alkekengi* (sometimes also listed as *P. franchetti*)
FAMILY	Solanaceae
& KNOWN AS	Alkekengi, winter cherry, strawberry tomato, and cape gooseberry (though this name is more often used for *Physalis peruviana*).
LIFE SPAN	Hardy perennial
HABITAT	Japan
APPEARANCE	Grows to a height of 18 inches (45 cm). Its stems are straight and its leaves large. Its whitish purple flowers, which appear in late summer, develop into large green pods, that turn deep orange as they ripen. Their texture is papery. It has creeping rhizomes.
SOIL	Plant in a well-cultivated, well-drained soil that is not acid or very rich.
LOCATION	Full sun.
PROPAGATION & CARE By Seed	Sow the seed 1/8 inch (3 mm) deep and maintain them at a temperature between 65° and 75°F (18° to 24°C). Do this in March, and you should get pods the first year. Transplant seedlings 12 inches (30 cm) apart into the garden, when you plant out tomatoes. <div align="center">**OR**</div> In milder climates, sow seed outdoors in May. Germination takes two to four weeks. Thin the seedlings when they are 2 inches (5 cm) high to a distance of 12 inches (30 cm) apart.
Vegetative	In early spring plants that are at least three years old can be dug and pieces of underground runners cut off and replanted 12 inches (30 cm) apart. Plants less than three years old will be unsuitable for use as propagative stock.
HARVESTING	When the pods start to change color from green to orange, cut the stems. If you harvest them while they are still quite green, the pods will shrivel up and fall off while they are drying.
DRYING	Tie them in small bunches, and either hang them upside

down, or stand them in jars in a dry, dark, well-ventilated place (Methods 1 or 2). When the stems and pods are quite dry, remove the leaves. The dry pods may be sprayed with clear plastic, which will preserve them indefinitely.

WARNING Do not grow *Physalis alkekengi* where its invasive runners will choke out other plant roots. It is much like mint in this regard, so choose its location carefully.

NOTE The cultivar *Physalis alkekengi* 'Gigantea' is taller than the species and produces larger pods.

COCKSCOMB

LATIN NAME	*Celosia cristata*
FAMILY	Amaranthaceae
LIFE SPAN	Half-hardy annual
HABITAT	Tropics
APPEARANCE	Dwarf varieties grow to a height of 12 inches (30 cm) and tall varieties to a height of 24 inches (60 cm). Its stems are stiff, upright, and branching, and its foliage is luxurious. Flowers are large and showy, and may be rose-pink, coral, salmon, purple, or yellow in color. Their texture and form is unusual. It blooms in mid- to late summer, depending on when the seeds were sown and how much warmth was available to them.
SOIL	Prefers a well-enriched, well-drained loamy soil.
LOCATION	Plant in full sun, sheltered from wind. It thrives in sun and heat, but not in a cool or wet summer.
PROPAGATION & CARE BY SEED	Sow the seed indoors as early as possible in the spring; barely covering it with the starting medium. It is *essential* to maintain a temperature between 65° and 75° F (18° and 24° C). Germination will take from seven to twelve days. When the seedlings are about 1 inch (2.5 cm) high, pot them individually into 3-inch pots. They will need a minimum temperature of 60° F (15° C) until it is time to harden them off. Harden off when the risk of frost is past and plant them out 12 inches (30 cm) apart when *all* risk of frost is over, and the nights are beginning to warm up (at the same time you plant out your sweet peppers). <center>**OR**</center>When the roots fill the 3-inch pots, pot them into 4-inch pots, and keep them at a minimum temperature of 60° F (15° C), as stated above, until it is time to harden them off. Syringe them twice daily with tepid water. They will thrive better in a greenhouse than the house. Follow the directions above for planting out.
HARVESTING	Cut the stem when they are just coming into full bloom. Do not strip off the leaves.

COCKSCOMB
Celosia cristata

DRYING Stand them alone or in small *uncrowded* bunches in a container with no water, when the stems are no longer moist, and hang them upside down in a dry, dark, warm place. It is most important to see that the stems are *completely free of moisture before hanging* them or the damp will damage the blooms.

NOTE The Plumosa Group of cultivars of *Celosia cristata* have feathery flower heads that are grown and treated in the same way. Their flowers are also very showy.

CUPID'S-DART
Catananche caerulea

CUPID'S-DART

LATIN NAME	*Catananche caerulea*
FAMILY	Compositae
& KNOWN AS	Blue succory, blue cupidone
LIFE SPAN	Hardy perennial, though somewhat short-lived
HABITAT	Western Mediterranean
APPEARANCE	Grows to a height of 24 inches (60 cm). The stems are wiry and flexible; leaves are gray-green and narrow. The flowers, which are a brilliant blue, are protected by silver, papery bracts. They bloom from June to August, after which they become everlasting silver-gray seed heads.
SOIL	Ordinary soil with good drainage.
LOCATION	Sunny, warm, and sheltered from winds, or the plants will need staking for support.
PROPAGATION & CARE **BY SEED**	Sow seed 1/8 inch (3 mm) deep outdoors in May and the plants will bloom the following summer. If you want to have flowers the first summer after sowing, plant the seed indoors 1/8 inch (3 mm) deep in March, keeping them at a temperature of 55° to 60° F (13° to 16° C). Prick out the seedlings into 3-inch pots when the first true leaves are just beginning to develop, and transplant 18 inches (45 cm) apart into the garden when the nights are beginning to warm up (a week to ten days after you plant out tomatoes).
VEGETATIVE	Take root cuttings early in the spring. Plant them in a cold frame. When a few leaves have developed plant in the garden 18 inches (45 cm) apart.
HARVESTING	Flowers can be cut when they are fully open. Because they close soon after midday, cut them in the morning. They may also be cut when still in bud, and will dry a beautiful silvery color.
DRYING	In either case, hang them to dry in a warm well-ventilated place (Methods 7 or 8). Allow some flowers to develop the goblet-shaped, silver-gray seed heads in the garden, then hang as above to dry.

ERYNGO
Eryngium spp

ERYNGO

LATIN NAME	*Eryngium* spp
FAMILY	Umbelliferae
& KNOWN AS	Sea holly is often used for several of these species, but according to *Hortus Third*, sea holly, sea holm, and sea eryngo are common names for *Eryngium martimum* only.

    ❧   ❧   ❧

Here I have digressed from the format I have used to describe the other thirty plants. There are several species of eryngo that dry well and though all of them have similar cultural, harvesting, and drying needs, the habitat and appearance of each species varies. This information is listed for each species separately, as well as the optimum distance plants should stand from each other.

    ❧   ❧   ❧

SOIL	A well-drained, light, sandy soil that has been adequately limed is best.
LOCATION	Full sun.
PROPAGATION & CARE BY SEED	Ideally the seed should be planted as soon as it is ripe (in the fall) at a depth of 1/8 inch (3 mm). At a temperature of 60° to 70° F (16° to 21° C), they will take at least three weeks to germinate and may take as long as six. The seedlings do not transplant well because the roots are thin and break easily. But by the time the plants are a year old it will be possible to transplant them.
VEGETATIVE	Mature roots can be divided in the spring. Root cuttings can also be taken and replanted 2 inches (5 cm) deep in a light sandy soil.
HARVESTING	Cutting should be left until the flower heads and stems have turned blue. If cut while still immature the stems will not remain stiff when they are dry. It may, therefore, be necessary to cut individual flower heads as they are ready. They will need wiring before drying.
DRYING	Dry the flowers and stems in an upright position (Method 2). Short stems can also be pushed into Oasis to dry

(Method 4). Another option is to arrange them in containers and leave them to dry in situ. If you want eryngo to turn an attractive brown, you can preserve it with glycerine (Method 15). Use mature (firm and succulent) stems, but not old (woody) ones. A few seed pods should be allowed to develop for drying.

THE SPECIES

E. alpinum   Native to the Swiss Alps. It grows from 20 to 23 inches (50 to 60 cm) high. The spreading heart-shaped leaves are toothed. The flowers that bloom in June and July, surrounded by leaflike bracts, are a brilliant shade of steely blue which often extends to the stems and upper leaves. Plants will eventually need 1 square foot (30 square cm) of space if they are not to become crowded.

E. bourgatti   Native to Spain. Growing to a height of 18 inches (45 cm), its divided blue-green leaves have prominent white veins. The flowers, a steely blue color, bloom in June and July. This species is sometimes known as Mediterranean sea holly and requires the same amount of space to grow as *E. alpinum*.

E. giganteum   Native to the Caucasus region. A short-lived perennial, it grows to a height of 4 feet (1.20 m) or more. The floral bracts are long-toothed and rigid, and the flowers that appear in July are a blue-gray color. It needs more space than most *Eryngiums,* so give each plant about 18 square inches (45 square cm) of space in which to grow.

E. maritimum   This is the wild sea holly found on the sandy shores of western Europe, the Mediterranean, and Britain. It grows to a height of 18 inches (45 cm) with glaucus, bluish, fleshy, stiff leaves; bears pale blue flowers during July and August. This species has become naturalized on the Atlantic coast of the United States. It needs as much space in which to grow as *E. giganteum*.

E. x oliverianum   A hybrid of uncertain parentage, which can vary in height from 3 feet (90 cm) to as much as 8 feet (2.4 m). The shorter varieties are more desirable. The leaves are deeply cut; the flowers are very decorative and a rich blue color. Plant it in the middle of a circle whose diameter is 4 feet (1.20 m).

E. planum	Native to Europe and Asia, it grows about 30 inches (75 cm) high. From July to August it bears many small, roundish, blue flower heads on tough stems. It needs at least 1 square foot (30 square cm) of space in which to grow.
NOTE	The flower heads of most species of *Eryngium* dry well. Because most of them have a multibranching habit, the natural stems of the flower heads are short. These stems are also very tough and cannot be wired when green (one species that can be wired green is *E. bourgatti*). To make different types of false stems, and to lengthen natural ones, see Wiring and Making False Stems, pages 152 to 157.

EVERLASTING SAND FLOWER
Ammobium alatum

EVERLASTING SAND FLOWER

LATIN NAME	*Ammobium alatum*
FAMILY	Compositae
& KNOWN AS	Winged everlasting
LIFE SPAN	Half-hardy annual
HABITAT	Australia
APPEARANCE	Grows to a height of 18 to 24 inches (45 to 60 cm). Its stems are stiff and the leaves oblong. Flowers are silvery white, often with a yellow center, and it blooms profusely from July to October.
SOIL	A light, rich, preferably sandy soil.
LOCATION	A warm sheltered spot with plenty of sun.
PROPAGATION & CARE BY SEED	Sow seed 1/8 inch (3 mm) deep indoors in March, where a temperature of 65° F (18° C) can be maintained. Or sow seed outdoors when there is no chance of another frost. Plant out indoor-sown seedlings when there is no chance of another frost, leaving 8 inches (20 cm) between plants. Or thin out outdoor-sown seedlings to stand at the same distance apart. Transplanting outdoor-sown seedlings is usually not successful.
HARVESTING	Picking time is critical if you want the flowers to be pure white when dry. They must be picked before the yellow centers are visible, but after the buds have started to open. If you want the yellow centers to show, the flowers should be picked when fully opened. Immature buds do not open once they are cut, so harvest the flowers with short stems in order to leave the buds to develop on the plants.
DRYING	The stems should be wired while they are still green. Air dry by hanging (Method 1) or use Oasis (Method 4).
NOTE	They can be used fresh as a cut flower, but do not make a particularly interesting subject for the flower border. There is a cultivar of everlasting sand flower that you will find listed as *Ammobium alatum* 'Grandiflora.' It has larger flowers than the species and is even more free flowering.

FEATHER GRASS, EUROPEAN
Stipa pennata

FEATHER GRASS, EUROPEAN

LATIN NAME	*Stipa pennata*
FAMILY	Gramineae
LIFE SPAN	Hardy perennial
HABITAT	Europe and Siberia
APPEARANCE	Grows to a height of 24 inches (60 cm). The leaves are narrow and light green. The silvery buff-colored plumes develop during the summer.
SOIL	It grows in any well-drained, fertile garden soil.
LOCATION	Dry, sunny spot.
PROPAGATION & CARE	Sow seed 1/8 inch (3 mm) deep when the ground has begun to warm up in spring, about the same time you sow beets.
BY SEED	OR Sow seed 1/8 inch (3 cm) deep in March, where the temperature can be maintained between 55° and 65° F (13° and 18° C). Plant these seedlings out in the garden about the same time you plant out tomatoes, spacing them 18 inches (45 cm) apart.
VEGETATIVE	In early spring when growth has just started, plants that are two or three years old can be dug and the tufted clumps divided. Replant 18 inches (45 cm) apart.
HARVESTING	Cut just as the heads have fully opened, but before the seeds mature.
DRYING	Tie in small bunches and hang upside down in a cool, dry, well-ventilated place (Method 1).

GLOBE AMARANTH
Gomphrena globosa

GLOBE AMARANTH

LATIN NAME	*Gomphrena globosa*
FAMILY	Amaranthaceae
& KNOWN AS	Globe everlasting, gomphrena, Spanish clover
LIFE SPAN	Half-hardy annual
HABITAT	India and the tropical areas of Australia, Southeast Asia, and the Americas
APPEARANCE	Grows to a height of about 18 inches (45 cm). Stems are stiff and upright, leaves are oblong. Its flowers may be white, rose, purple, salmon, or orange-bronze, and are not unlike clover flowers. Blooms from July to September, dying with the first frost.
SOIL	Plant in a light, well-drained, humus-rich soil. It appreciates manure, too.
LOCATION	A warm sunny spot.
PROPAGATION & CARE BY SEED	In March, sow seed indoors keeping them at a temperature of 75° F (24° C). The seed should be barely covered. They will germinate in two to three weeks. When the seedlings are about 1-inch (2.5 cm) high, transplant them into 3-inch pots. When they have four to six leaves, transplant them into a 4-inch pot. They now need a temperature of at least 60° F (15° C), preferably around 70° F (21° C). Transplant them once more into 5-inch pots and give them plenty of light. In cooler climates they should be grown in a greenhouse because they need a minimum summer temperature of 55° F (13° C). Syringe the foliage at least once a day in the greenhouse. If your summers are warm, they may be planted out from their 4-inch pots a week to ten days after the last frost, and when the nights are beginnng to warm up (about the same time as you plant out sweet peppers). Plant them in the garden 8 inches (20 cm) apart.
HARVESTING	Cut the flowers when their globe shape has fully developed and their color is at its most intense. If left in the garden until they are mature they will shatter when dried. Remove the

foliage when the plants have been freshly cut. If you wish to reinforce the stems with wire, do it while the material is fresh.

Dry, if possible, in the dark, by Method 7 or 8. Or you can cut each flower with a 2-inch (5-cm) stem and wire the heads individually, then dry them by Methods 4, 5, 6, 9, or 10.

NOTE Some mail-order nurseries list the different colors of globe amaranth separately.

There is also the species *Gomphrena haageana*, which is bright orange. It is grown in the same way as *G. globosa*.

GLOBE THISTLE, SMALL

LATIN NAME	*Echinops ritro*
FAMILY	Compositae
LIFE SPAN	Hardy perennial
HABITAT	Southern Europe
APPEARANCE	Grows to a height of 36 to 48 inches (90 cm to 1.20 m). The tough leaves are covered with a cottonlike down, and are coarse and grayish green. The flower heads are quite spherical and vary from deep blue to steel color. The plant may flower any time between June and August.
SOIL	Prefers a fairly heavy, well-limed, well-drained soil.
LOCATION	A warm and sunny spot.
PROPAGATION & CARE BY SEED	Sow seed 1/4 inch (6 mm) deep in early summer where a temperature of about 60° F (16° C) can be maintained. Plant out these seedlings when they are 2 inches (5 cm) high. They should stand 24 inches (60 cm) apart.
VEGETATIVE	In late fall or early spring, plants that are at least three years old may be dug up, divided, and replanted 24 inches (60 cm) apart.
HARVESTING	Cut the plants from late summer until frost, before the metallic blue bracts have fully opened. Remove the coarse basal leaves, but keep a few of the others on; when dry, they will turn a clear gray.
DRYING	It is the round thistle heads, however, that are the most desirable part of the plant for winter decoration. Cut them with a length of stem and hang each head individually, upside down, in a dry, dark, well-ventilated place (Method 1). They can also be preserved in silica gel by Method 11. The heads can be given a touch of silver or gold paint.
NOTE	These plants make an unusual fresh-cut flower. Be sure to cut the head before it is in full bloom, or the early florets will quickly turn brown. This is a plant that bees love.

GLOBE THISTLE, SMALL
Echinops ritro

HARE'S-TAIL GRASS
Lagurus ovatus

HARE'S-TAIL GRASS

LATIN NAME	*Lagurus ovatus*
FAMILY	Gramineae
& KNOWN AS	Hare's tail, rabbit-tail grass
LIFE SPAN	Hardy annual
HABITAT	The Mediterranean region of southern Europe; has also become naturalized in Southern England, Australia, and South Africa.
APPEARANCE	Grows to a height of 12 inches (30 cm). A compact, tidy plant with firm stems and flat leaves. The egg-shaped, silky heads turn from greenish white to creamy white. It blooms prolifically from midsummer to first frost.
SOIL	Grows well in any cultivated garden soil.
LOCATION	Prefers a sunny spot.
PROPAGATION & CARE BY SEED	Sow seed outdoors in the spring: 1/4 inch (6 mm) deep in the spot where you want the plants to grow (about the same time you sow your first beets). When the seedlings are about 2 inches (5 cm) high, thin them to stand 12 inches (30 cm) apart.
HARVESTING	Cut the stems just as the heads have become fully open, but before the seeds mature (the leaves may be left on or taken off).
DRYING	Tie them in small bunches and hang them upside down in a dry, well-ventilated place (Method 1). They will retain their silvery tone and downy texture when dry.

HEATHER

LATIN NAME	*Calluna vulgaris*
FAMILY	Ericaceae
& KNOWN AS	Scotch heather, ling
LIFE SPAN	Hardy perennial
HABITAT	Great Britain, Scandinavia. Though not found wild in North America, it will grow where the climate is temperate and the soil suitable.
APPEARANCE	Varying in height from 3 inches (7.5 cm) to 36 inches (90 cm), this evergreen shrub has small narrow leaves. Flowers appear in August and September in the axils of the leaves on the upper stems. Colors range from white through to pink and purple, depending on the variety.
SOIL	An acid soil is essential. It can be enriched with peat or leaf compost, and must be quite free of lime.
LOCATION	Will tolerate a moist situation; likes full sun.
PROPAGATION & CARE	Plants can be divided in spring or fall, or tip cuttings can be taken in early summer.
VEGETATIVE	Plants should be set about 18 inches (45 cm) apart.
HARVESTING	Gather the stems before the blooms are fully developed. The foliage need not be removed, unless you wish.
DRYING	Hang to dry using either Method 1, 7, or 8. Preserve the foliage in glycerine (Method 15) or the flowers by pressing (Method 16).
NOTE	There are many species and varieties of heather. In suitable soil and under favorable climatic conditions, it is possible to have blooms every month of the year.

HEATHER
Calluna vulgaris

HONESTY
Lunaria annua

HONESTY

LATIN NAME	*Lunaria annua* (occasionally known also as *L. biennis*)
FAMILY	Cruciferae
& KNOWN AS	Silver dollar (for *L. annua*); money flower, satin flower, moonwort (all for the genus *Lunaria*)
LIFE SPAN	Hardy biennial
HABITAT	Europe
APPEARANCE	Grows to a height of 24 to 36 inches (60 to 90 cm). The erect stems bear broad pointed leaves. Flowers are mauve and bloom in early summer. The seedpods are flat and almost circular, about the size of a silver dollar. Under the greenish brown or purple paperlike covering is a silvery disc.
SOIL	Ordinary, well-drained soil that has been cultivated and composted for a previous crop. An overrich soil will produce an excess of foliage, at the expense of a heavy crop of flowers and successive seedpods.
LOCATION	Will tolerate some shade.
PROPAGATION & CARE By Seed	Plant seed 1/4 inch (6 mm) deep in early spring where a temperature of 60° to 70° F (16° to 21° C) can be maintained. Germination will occur in 5 to 10 days. These seedlings can be transplanted into the garden 12 inches (30 cm) apart at the same time you plant out tomatoes. This planting should give you a late crop of pods the same summer. <center>OR</center> Sow seed directly in the ground 1/4 inch (6 mm) deep in early summer; they will germinate in 15 to 20 days. When the seedlings are 2 inches (5 cm) high, thin them to stand 12 inches (30 cm) apart. These thinned plants will transplant. This sowing will not flower until early the following summer. Leave a few pods to ripen and self-sow for future crops.
HARVESTING	Cut the stems at whatever length you desire when the seedpods are beginning to dry, but before the seeds turn yellow.
DRYING	Tie in bunches and hang them to dry in a cool dry place (Method 1). In about three or four weeks the pods should

be completely dry, and the outer skins can be rubbed off between your thumb and forefinger to expose the silver disc underneath. These discs can be spray painted. Young green pods can be preserved in glycerine (Method 15).

NOTE | There is a purple variety of this species, but it is less useful in winter bouquets and is not a particularly interesting plant in the flower garden.

IMMORTELLE
Xeranthemum annuum

IMMORTELLE

LATIN NAME	*Xeranthemum annuum*
FAMILY	Compositae
& KNOWN AS	Xeranthemum, annual everlasting
LIFE SPAN	Hardy annual
HABITAT	Southern Europe
APPEARANCE	Grows to a height of 18 to 24 inches (45 to 60 cm). Stems are strong and wiry, and its narrow, pale green leaves are covered with down.
	The flowers, which bloom continuously from midsummer until early fall (light frost does them no harm), range in color from white, pink, and rose to violet and purple. They may be double or single.
SOIL	Will grow in any ordinary garden soil with good drainage.
LOCATION	Full sun is essential.
PROPAGATION & CARE By Seed	Sow them in the open garden, preferably where you want them to bloom, 1/8 inch (3 mm) deep, in late spring when the ground has warmed up (the same time you sow beets). **OR** Sow seed indoors 1/8 inch (3 mm) deep in early spring at a temperature of about 65° F (18° C). Germination will occur in ten to twenty days. Plant out the seedlings, after hardening them off, about two to three weeks before you plant out tomatoes; light frost is unlikely to damage them. They should be thinned or planted out 12 inches (30 cm) apart.
HARVESTING	Cut the stems as long as possible. Flowers can be cut at various stages, from half open buds to fully open flowers; they retain their color for a long time when dried.
DRYING	The leaves may be stripped off before or after drying. The flowers and stems should be hung in small bunches in a dry, dark, well-ventilated place (Method 1). They can also be dried in Oasis (Method 4).

JOB'S-TEARS
Coix lacyrma-jobi

JOB'S-TEARS

LATIN NAME	*Coix lacyrma-jobi*
FAMILY	Gramineae
LIFE SPAN	Half-hardy annual
HABITAT	Tropical parts of Asia
APPEARANCE	Grows to a height of 24 to 36 inches (60 to 90 cm). It is a coarse grass with large, pearly, silver-gray seedpods that hang from its many stems. These seedpods appear between late summer and the first frost.
SOIL	Light, rich, and well drained.
LOCATION	A warm and sunny spot.
PROPAGATION & CARE BY SEED	In early spring, sow seed indoors at a depth of 1/2 inch (1 cm) deep; maintain them at a temperature of about 65° F (18° C). Seeds will germinate in ten to twenty days. Seedlings can be transplanted outside when all danger of frost is past. OR Where springs are mild, plant seed 1/2 inch (1 cm) deep in late April in the spot that you want the plants to flower. When seedlings are about 2 inches (5 cm) high, thin plants to 18 inches (45 cm) apart.
HARVESTING	Start cutting in late summer, as soon as the seedpods have fully formed. The earlier cuttings will have green stems, the later ones beige.
DRYING	They need no drying, but store them upright in cans or jars in a dry dark place. Fully dried, they will last up to two years.
NOTE	The seedpods can be threaded to make attractive necklaces.

LOVE-LIES-BLEEDING
Amaranthus caudatus

LOVE-LIES-BLEEDING

LATIN NAME	*Amaranthus caudatus*
FAMILY	Amaranthaceae
& KNOWN AS	Tassel flower, foxtail, chenille, velvet flower
LIFE SPAN	Half-hardy annual
HABITAT	Tropical Asia and Africa
APPEARANCE	Grows to a height of 24 inches (60 cm) or more. Its main stem is thick, sturdy, and branching. The large, light green leaves are carried on reddish stems. The pendant plumes are a rich red and bloom through the summer until the first frost.
SOIL	Light, well-limed, humus-rich, well-drained soil is preferred.
LOCATION	Full sun, sheltered from wind. It thrives in a hot dry place.
PROPAGATION & CARE By Seed	For early pluming, sow seed indoors during early spring where a temperature between 65° and 75° F (18° and 24° C) can be maintained. Seed should be barely covered and will germinate in two to three weeks. Harden off the resultant seedlings and plant them out at least ten days after your last frost date 24 inches (60 cm) apart.
HARVESTING	The flower spikes should be cut before the seeds begin to ripen. The first cut should be made so that the flower buds are left to develop for a later crop.
DRYING	Hang upside down to dry in a warm, dry, dark place (Methods 1, 7, or 8).
NOTE	When dried, love-lies-bleeding retains its color well and lasts a long time, but in addition it makes an impressive fresh-cut flower. There is a variety with pale green plumes usually listed under the name *Amaranthus caudatus viridis*, which also dries well.

PAMPAS GRASS
Cortaderia selloana

PAMPAS GRASS

LATIN NAME	*Cortaderia selloana* (occasionally known also as *C. argentea*)
FAMILY	Gramineae
LIFE SPAN	Hardy perennial
HABITAT	South America, especially Brazil, Argentina, and Chile
APPEARANCE	Growing to a height of 60 to 80 inches (1.50 to 2.00 m), this stately grass has very narrow, stiff, and rough-edged leaves. The showy, silky white plumes appear from late summer to early winter. The male and female plumes are carried on different plants with the female plumes being more desirable for decoration. The male plant has an awn or bristle-like appendage.
SOIL	A rich, light, and sandy soil suits it best.
LOCATION	A sheltered spot, in full sun.
PROPAGATION & CARE BY SEED	Sow seed 1/8 inch (3 mm) deep, where a temperature of 55° to 65° F (13° to 18° C) can be maintained, in very early spring. Transplant to a nursery bed in late spring, and plant into the garden at the end of summer. Mature plants will need a distance of 60 to 72 inches (1.50 to 1.80 m) between them. Keep the plants well watered in dry weather. In spring, before growth starts afresh, trim or burn off mature clumps to clean them up.
VEGETATIVE	Once female plants are established, they should be propagated vegetatively. Mature plants can be divided in the spring, just as the first signs of growth are showing. Replant them 60 to 70 inches (1.50 to 1.80 m) apart.
HARVESTING	If you cut the plumes when they are well budded, but before they explode, they will fluff out and not fall apart when they dry.
DRYING	Dry them in the sun (Method 2) for two or three days, but take them into a dry place at night. They can also be preserved in glycerine (Method 15). If they are not to be used for decoration at once, store them either in a cool dry place in a tall container or lay them on a clean shelf. Do not crowd the plumes.

WARNING	Always wear gloves when handling pampas grass: the leaf edges are very sharp.
NOTE	*Cortaderia selloana* can be obtained in a variety of colors, including gold, silver, and pink, and it has plumes that are either shaggy, feathery, or cloudy.

PEARL GRASS

LATIN NAME	*Briza maxima*
FAMILY	Gramineae
& KNOWN AS	Big quaking grass
LIFE SPAN	Hardy annual
HABITAT	Mediterranean region
APPEARANCE	Grows to a height of 18 inches (45 cm). The leaves are bright green and flat; the stems are delicate and erect. In early summer the flowers develop into strange, nodding, heart-shaped spikelets that last until September.
SOIL	Grows well in any cultivated garden soil.
LOCATION	An open sunny place.
PROPAGATION & CARE BY SEED	Sow the seed 1/8 inch (3 mm) deep in spring where the plants are going to flower. In climates where winters are mild, seed may be sown in September. *Do not transplant seedlings* because the roots are delicate and will be reluctant to reestablish themselves in a new location. When the plants are 2 inches (5 cm) high, thin them to stand 6 to 9 inches (15 to 22 cm) apart.
HARVESTING	Cut the stems as long as possible when the weather is dry, and when the spikelets are almost fully developed, but before the seeds mature.
DRYING	Tie them in small bunches. Hang upside down in a dry, cool, well-ventilated place (Method 1).
NOTE	*B. minor* is known as little quaking grass. It is grown in exactly the same way as pearl grass and is also very ornamental.

Pearl Grass
Briza maxima

Pearly Everlasting
Anaphalis margaritacea

PEARLY EVERLASTING

LATIN NAME	*Anaphalis margaritacea*
FAMILY	Compositae
& KNOWN AS	Life-everlasting
LIFE SPAN	Hardy perennial
HABITAT	Widespread in North America, eastern Asia
APPEARANCE	Grows to a height of 12 to 16 inches (30 to 40 cm). Leaves are silvery gray and woolly underneath. Flowers heads are white, small, and dense, and they bloom in late summer.
SOIL	Will thrive in any soil, even a poor one, as long as it is very well drained.
LOCATION	Sun or partial shade. The less sun it has, the more important adequate drainage becomes.
PROPAGATION & CARE BY SEED	Sow seed 1/8 inch (3 mm) deep in early spring in a sheltered seedbed or cold frame, where a temperature of 60° F (16° C) can be maintained—choose a sheltered location or use a cold frame if necessary. When the seedlings are about 2 inches (5 cm) high, plant them 12 inches (30 cm) apart in a nursery bed. In the fall, plant them into their permanent position 18 inches (45 cm) apart.
VEGETATIVE	Two-year-old (or older) plants may be dug and divided in early spring. Such plants may also be dug and divided in the fall where winters are mild. Basal shoots can be detached from the plants in late spring and rooted in sand.
HARVESTING	Before the flowers are fully mature, and long before the seed starts to form, cut the stems as long as possible. Or pick individual flowers with 2-inch (5-cm) stems; while they are still fresh make bunches of six or eight flower heads.
DRYING	Remove the foliage from long stems and hang in a cool, dry, well-ventilated place (Method 1). At this stage there will be less chance of the stems bending and the heads flopping over like a shepherd's crook. Little flower bunches will need a wire stem that can be made before or after drying the flower heads (see the section on Wiring, page 156). If this is done while the flowers are fresh, the wire stem can then be

pushed into Oasis and the flowers allowed to dry. If the wiring is not done when they are fresh, the bunches of flower heads will have to be dried by hanging (Method 1); they can then be wired.

NOTE | *Anaphalis triplinervis* is a similar species that can be found in seed catalogs.

PINK POKERS
Psylliostachys suworowii

Pink Pokers

LATIN NAME	*Psylliostachys suworowii* (sometimes listed also as *Limonium suworowii* and *Statice suworowii*)
FAMILY	Plumbaginaceae
& KNOWN AS	Candlewick statice
LIFE SPAN	Half-hardy annual
HABITAT	Turkestan
APPEARANCE	Grows to a height of 18 inches (45 cm). The branching ribbed stems rise from a basal rosette of midgreen leaves. The rose-pink flowers are packed in long, narrow, dense spikes, some of which grow straight; others encircle the plant. They bloom from mid- to late summer.
SOIL	Any ordinary, well-drained garden soil.
LOCATION	An open sunny place.
PROPAGATION & CARE **BY SEED**	Start seed indoors as early as possible in the spring. Sow the seed 1/4 inch (6 cm) deep, where a temperature of 65° to 75° F (18° to 24° C) can be maintained. Germination takes ten to twenty days. When the first true leaves have developed, transplant the seedlings into 3-inch pots. Harden them off before planting them outdoors (at the same time you plant out tomatoes) 18 inches (45 cm) apart. **OR** In milder climates, sow seed at the same depth, where the plants will flower, during the late spring, and after all risk of frost is passed. Thin to 18 inches (45 cm) apart. This method will delay flowering, so do not use it unless your area typically has a long, mild, *dry* fall.
HARVESTING	Cut the flower stems as long as possible when the flowers are fully open to the tips of the blossom.
DRYING	Tie them in small bunches and hang in a warm, dark, dry, well-ventilated place (Method 7 or 8).
NOTE	*P. suworowii* may suffer from gray mold, which causes a gray fungus to appear on the stems and flowers. To prevent it, give them plenty of room and avoid overhead watering.

SAFFLOWER
Carthamus tinctorius

SAFFLOWER

LATIN NAME	*Carthamus tinctorius*
FAMILY	Compositae
& KNOWN AS	Dyer's saffron, bastard saffron, Dyer's or Distaff thistle, false saffron
LIFE SPAN	Hardy annual
HABITAT	There seems to be some disagreement among the experts as to where safflower originated. It grows well in any temperate climate, as well as Egypt, parts of China and India, and most of Europe.
APPEARANCE	Grows to a height of 2 to 3 feet (60 to 90 cm). The stiff upright stems branch at the top and the oval-shaped leaves are prickly. The thistlelike flowers, which first appear in midsummer, are a deep orange-yellow; the period of bloom is short. The fruit, often incorrectly referred to as the seed, resembles pearly white shells.
SOIL	Ordinary well-drained soil.
LOCATION	Full sun.
PROPAGATION & CARE BY SEED	The seed is large and can be sown outdoors 1/4 inch (6 cm) deep in late spring when the temperature is about 60° F (15° C). Seed will germinate in about fourteen days. Seedlings do not transplant successfully. Thin them to stand 10 inches (25 cm) apart and keep the soil well cultivated.
HARVESTING	The flowers can be picked when still green and closed, or left on the plant until the florets are showing plenty of color.
DRYING	The stems will stay stiff, so they can either be arranged in Oasis (Method 4) and left to dry or can be dried upright (Method 2).

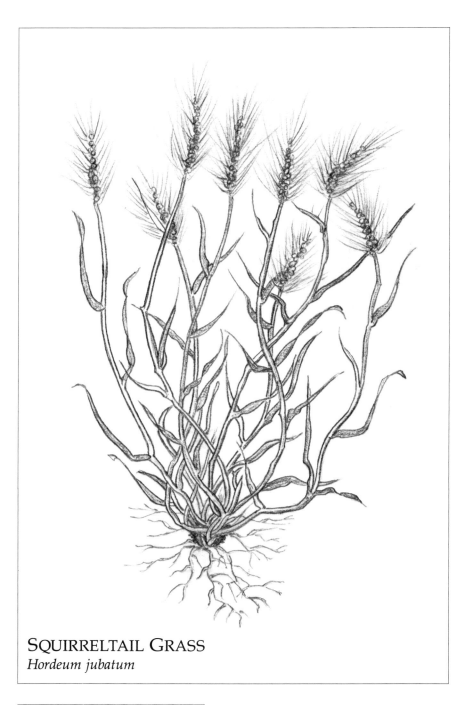

SQUIRRELTAIL GRASS
Hordeum jubatum

SQUIRRELTAIL GRASS

LATIN NAME	*Hordeum jubatum*
FAMILY	Gramineae
& KNOWN AS	Foxtail barley, squirreltail barley
LIFE SPAN	Hardy annual
HABITAT	North and South America, Siberia
APPEARANCE	Growing to a height of 18 inches (45 cm), this barleylike grass has narrow leaves. Its short, finely bearded heads appear in June and last until September.
SOIL	Not particular about the type of soil, but it does need a well-drained one.
LOCATION	A dry open situation and some sun.
PROPAGATION & CARE **BY SEED**	In early spring sow the seed 1/8 inch (3 mm) deep where the plants are to flower and where the temperature is about 55° to 60° F (13° to 15° C). Does not transplant well. When the seedlings are about 2 inches (5 cm) high, thin them out to stand 12 inches (30 cm) apart.
HARVESTING	Cut the stems before the bearded heads have fully ripened.
DRYING	Tie in small bunches and hang in a dry well-ventilated place (Method 1).

STARFLOWER
Scabiosa stellata

STARFLOWER

LATIN NAME	*Scabiosa stellata*
FAMILY	Dipsacaceae
& KNOWN AS	Scabious paper moon, scabiosa starball
LIFE SPAN	Hardy annual
HABITAT	Western Mediterranean region
APPEARANCE	Grows to a height of about 24 inches (60 cm). The leaves are feathery and the soft lavender-colored flowers are hemispherical. When the petals fall off you will have "striking round heads of starlike pistils, suspended by delicate, cuplike calyxes," as one of my seed catalogs describes this fascinating flower. The flowers are greenish beige. The stems are stiff and strong.
SOIL	Prefers a well-limed light soil with good drainage.
LOCATION	Full sun, though it will tolerate some shade.
PROPAGATION & CARE By Seed	In late spring, the seed can be sown 1/4 inch (6 cm) deep where the plants are to grow. The seeds are large, so they can be sown individually about 12 inches (30 cm) apart. Then it will not be necessary to thin the young plants. OR Start them indoors in pots where a temperature of about 60° F (15° C) can be maintained. The seed should germinate in about ten days. Plant out 12 inches (30 cm) apart. Keep the soil well cultivated, otherwise no special care is needed.
HARVESTING	Do not delay the cutting once the petals have fallen or the heads will become very brittle.
DRYING	Little drying is necessary, but it should be done upright (Method 2 or 4).
NOTE	A coat of clear Krylon will prevent the flower heads from shattering and will lengthen the life of the dried heads (see page 204 for instructions on how to spray preservatives on dried-plant material).

STATICE
Limonium sinuatum

STATICE

LATIN NAME	*Limonium sinuatum*
FAMILY	Plumbaginaceae
& KNOWN AS	Sea lavender, marsh rosemary
LIFE SPAN	Biennial/perennial; grow as half-hardy annual
HABITAT	Mediterranean
APPEARANCE	Grows to a height of 36 inches (90 cm). Its leaves are rough, leathery, and deeply lobed. Blooming from midsummer to fall, the clusters of tiny flowers may be blue, yellow, rose, or white. Some seed catalogs offer unusual colors, including salmon-pink, orange-yellow, and pink-carmine.
SOIL	A well-drained loamy soil that is not acid and has not been recently manured.
LOCATION	Full sun.
PROPAGATION & CARE By Seed	Before sowing the seeds, it will be necessary to separate them—they often come in little clumps in the seed packet. Sow the seed indoors in spring, as early as possible, 1/4 inch (6 cm.) deep, where a temperature of 65° to 75° F (18° to 24° C) can be maintained. Germination will occur in ten to twenty days. When the first true leaves have developed, transplant the seedlings into 3-inch pots. Harden them off before planting them outdoors, at the same time you plant out your tomatoes, 18 inches (45 cm) apart.
	OR
	In milder climates, sow the seed 1/4 inch (6 cm) deep, where the plants will flower, in late spring, after all risk of frost has passed. Thin to 18 inches (45 cm) apart. This method will delay flowering, so do not use it unless your area typically has a long, mild, *dry* fall.
HARVESTING	Cut the flowers when most of the blooms are at least three-quarters open. The foliage need not be removed.
DRYING	Hang them in a dark, dry, well-ventilated place (Method 1). You can also dry them upright (Method 2) or small pieces can be dried in Oasis (Method 4). If you want the flowers

	to be less brittle you can preserve them in a glycerine solution (Method 15).
NOTE	There are a number of other *Limonium* species whose flowers are suitable for drying.
L. bonduellii	A half-hardy annual that has yellow flowers. Cut when they are mature and hang to dry (Method 1).
L. latifolium	A hardy perennial, which has small lavender-blue flowers in the wild. It is possible to get specific varieties that are deep blue or violet from seed catalogs. Propagation can be done by seed or division of roots, but the former method is preferred because the roots do not like to be disturbed. This plant will not flower heavily until the second summer after seeding. Pick the flowers when they are in full bloom and the weather is dry. Dry them in an upright position (Method 2 or 4).
L. puberlum	A miniature half-hardy perennial suitable for growing as a potted plant. The color of the flowers varies from white to violet.
L. tataricum	More often found under the Latin name *Goniolimon tataricum*. A hardy perennial with lavender-colored flowers that fall off when dried. The white calyxes that remain after flower petals fall are dainty. Be sure that all the flowers are fully open before cutting them. They can be hung upside down to dry (Method 1), upright (Method 2), or small pieces can be cut off and pushed into Oasis to dry (Method 4). All the *Limonium* species mentioned above can also be used as fresh-cut flowers. The color of all the *Limoniums* tends to fade more quickly than many other everlasting flowers, so you will need to dry fresh ones every year.

STRAWFLOWER

LATIN NAME	*Helichrysum bracteatum*
FAMILY	Compositae
& KNOWN AS	Everlasting, immortelle, yellow paper daisy
LIFE SPAN	Half-hardy annual
HABITAT	Australia
APPEARANCE	Height varies from 12 inches (30 cm) to 36 inches (90 cm). The stems are firm and upright. The flowers come in a wide range of colors: white, yellow, pink, crimson, and bronze. Blooms start in midsummer and each plant may bear as many as thirty flowers. They will bloom until frost, but a rainy fall will damage them.
SOIL	Grows well in a fairly heavy loam that contains plenty of compost.
LOCATION	Full sun, in the warmest spot you can find; sheltered from winds.
PROPAGATION & CARE [BY SEED]	Sow the seed 1/8 inch (3 mm) deep in March, where a temperature of 60° to 65° F (16° to 18° C) can be maintained. The seed should germinate in ten to fifteen days. In most climates this will mean an indoor sowing. Harden off the seedlings and plant them out when all danger of frost is past. Plant them 12 inches (30 cm) apart. It is most important to give the plants a long season of growth, or they will not mature in time to be cut before fall rains.
HARVESTING	Cut the flower stems before the yellow centers are visible. They may also be cut in the bud stage. Remove the foliage whenever you cut them.
DRYING	You can either remove the heads while they are still green and put them on artificial wire stems, as commercial growers and florists do. Or you can tie the stems (flower heads still on) into small bunches and hang them upside down in

STRAWFLOWER
Helichrysum bracteatum

a dark, cool, well-ventilated place (Method 1).

When you are ready to use them, the stems can be threaded into straws or the hollow stems of other plants.

NOTE | Strawflowers make an excellent fresh-cut flower.

TEASEL
Dipsacus sativus

TEASEL

LATIN NAME	*Dipsacus sativus*
FAMILY	Dipsacaceae
LIFE SPAN	Hardy biennial
HABITAT	This variety is known only in cultivation. It is thought to be a variety that is a native of Europe and now naturalized in North America. See Note below.
APPEARANCE	Grows to a height of 48 to 60 inches (1.20 to 1.50 m). Its stems are rigid, prickly, and furrowed. The form of the lower leaves is curious: they are joined around the stem to form a basin that will hold water. Blooming in early summer, the lavender-colored flowers are followed by heads of hooked prickles.
SOIL	A rich moist soil.
LOCATION	Sun or part shade.
PROPAGATION & CARE **By SEED**	Sow the seed 1/4 inch (6 mm) deep in early summer, when the ground temperature reaches at least 60° F (16° C). Seedlings do not transplant well, so sow where they are to grow. Germination will take one to two weeks. Remember that this plant is a biennial, so flowers or seed will not be produced until the year after the seed is sown.
HARVESTING	Cut the heads after the flowers have withered. Remove the leaves and prickles.
DRYING	Stand upright to dry (Method 2). The heads can be sprayed with paint if you wish. While still green, cut and preserve the heads in glycerine (Method 15).
NOTE	Grieve's *Modern Herbal* (1931) says: ''Many botanists consider the Fuller's Teazle only a variety of the common wild Teazle, in which the spines of the flower heads are strongly developed into a hooked form, a feature preserved by cultivation, and apt to disappear by neglect, or on poor soil, causing it to relapse into the ordinary wild variety.'' These ''strongly developed hooks'' are used to tease cloth to raise the nap. The cultivation of teasels (or teazles) for use by British cloth makers was once a big business.

YARROW
Achillea filipendulina

YARROW

LATIN NAME	*Achillea filipendulina*
FAMILY	Compositae
LIFE SPAN	Hardy perennial
HABITAT	Temperate regions of northern Europe and Asia
APPEARANCE	Depending on the variety, it grows from 30 to 60 inches (75 cm to 1.50 m) high. Stems are erect and leaves fernlike. Its flowers are yellow, and grouped in flattened terminal clusters, that bloom from mid- to late summer.
SOIL	Any well-drained soil, and will even tolerate drought conditions.
LOCATION	Full sun. It will tolerate half shade in a dry location.
PROPAGATION & CARE BY SEED	Plant seed outdoors 1/4 inch (6 cm) deep, in early spring at the same time you plant your first carrots. They should germinate in ten to fifteen days. Transplant the seedlings when they are about 2 inches (5 cm) high into their permanent positions, 24 inches (60 cm) apart. Plants will not flower until the following year. If you have difficulty germinating seed outdoors, because of climatic conditions, plant some indoors (at the same depth), where a temperature of 70° F (21° C) can be maintained. They will germinate in five to seven days. Harden off the seedlings before planting them out in the garden some time during late spring or early summer.
VEGETATIVE	The plants should be divided every three years, either in the spring or early fall. You can also propagate them by cutting off pieces of the creeping underground rootstock and replanting them 24 inches (60 cm) apart.
HARVESTING	Cut the stems when the flowers are fully open. The terminal flattened clusters should still be firm to the touch. Do not remove the foliage.
DRYING	Hang individual stems to dry in a cool, dark, well-ventilated place (Method 1) or dry them upright (Method 2). The stems will toughen as they dry, so arrange other fresh material in whatever way you wish and let the yarrow dry in situ.

	NOTE
A. filipendul-ina	'Golden Cloth' is the best yellow yarrow.
A. mille-folium rosea	Common names are milfoil, sanguinary, and nose-bleed. The cultivar 'Cerise Queen' needs to be dried quickly when the flowers are mature. Use Method 7 or 8.
A. ptarmica	Known by the common name sneezewort or sneezeweed, it has double white flowers and doesn't always come true from seed. Try to obtain 'The Pearl' cultivar because it dries well and is more likely to come true from seed. It should be dried by Method 7 or 8.
WARNING	The roots of all yarrows spread rapidly underground. Plant it where it will not choke out less robust plants.

PART II

METHODS
OF
DRYING & PRESERVING
PLANT MATERIAL

Illustrations by Kay Gough and Judy Eliason

Be sure that all the material you dry is in perfect condition when picked. It is a waste of time to use odd bits and pieces, overmature flowers, or material that has become faded and droopy. If you do, the plants that you dry and/or preserve will be very disappointing. Also be sure that all plant materials are *quite* dry when they are gathered. Pick them in the late morning or the early afternoon after they have had a few hours of sunshine; preferably after two or three consecutive sunny days.

Remove at least some of the foliage, unless otherwise indicated in the species descriptions, before you begin a chosen drying process. If the leaves are thick, or there are too many of them, the drying process will be slowed down and the quality of the final product will suffer. If some foliage is unattractive when it has been dried make a note in your records and next time remove it before drying.

AIR DRYING

METHODS 1-4

IN THE FIRST PART of this book I have indicated the best air drying methods for each flower and grass described. What follows is a more detailed, step-by-step guide to these methods.

You will need an area in your home that is dry, well ventilated, and where as much light as possible can be excluded. Complete darkness is preferred. Clean air, free of dust and grease, is essential, as is an environment in which temperature can be controlled at a point of not less than 50°F (10°C). An attic, a basement, a spare bedroom, a cupboard under the stairs, a clothes closet, or even a recess (from which light can be excluded) are all suitable places. A kitchen cupboard is not recommended because plant material might pick up grease.

It is difficult to estimate how much time will be needed to dry any specific plant material because the preservation of plants is more an art than a science. So much depends on its thickness and moisture content as well as your drying conditions. By following one of the recommended methods two to three weeks should be sufficient.

If, after a few days, the hanging plant material is not beginning to dry it is a sign that the air is too damp. You may need to use some warmth to evaporate the moisture. A fan-forced electric heater with a thermostat set on LOW will help. Or you may find that a gentle air current from an ordinary electric fan is enough. Don't direct the breeze onto delicate material.

It has been suggested that because drying flowers are so attractive they should be hung in the living room. Because it is unlikely that your living room will be permanently dark, this is not advised. Dried in the light, the color of the flowers is likely to fade. Sunlight filtered through glass may bleach them completely.

AIR DRYING BY HANGING
METHOD 1

Gather the material to be dried into small bunches. Be sure that the heads of the flowers are at different levels—crowding will crush them and also prevent the air from circulating freely. Hang large flower heads individually for the same reasons.

Secure the stems in these bunches with rubber bands. As the stems dry and shrink the bands will tighten. As you put the rubber bands around the stems slip a plastic-covered twist tie (about 4 inches [10 cm] long) through the rubber bands and twist it to create a loop from which the bunch can be hung (Figure 1). If you use string, tie with a slip knot; this will have to be adjusted as the stems dry and shrink. Similarly, if you tie the stems with wire, you will have to tighten it quite often. The use of string or wire requires greater vigilance than rubber bands because the plant material may slip out and become damaged if it is not checked often to be certain it's secure.

Attach the bunches to be hang dried by the twist tie to either a wire, rope, or string and hang them in your drying area or from the bars of an old-fashioned wooden rack for drying clothes. Small bunches of flowers can be hung from wire clothes hangers and these can be hung on the rail of an empty clothes closet. Incidentally, this rail is an ideal place for hanging large individual flowers.

UPRIGHT, IN CONTAINERS WITHOUT WATER
METHOD 2

One of the most suitable, and certainly the cheapest, containers for air drying plant material in an upright position is a tall (40 ounce) juice can. Weight a juice can with stones or sand before you begin so that it doesn't tip over. Stretch chicken wire over the mouth of whatever container you use. Insert the plant stem or stems through the hole(s) in the wire (Figure 2). Don't crowd them. Then leave the plants to dry in your warm, dark, and well-ventilated place.

Most grasses will dry well in this way and by varying the height of the containers in your drying area, some of the stems will bend a little, making them appear more natural.

All *Allium* and *Limonium* species dry well by this method, as does pampas grass (*Cortaderia selloana*).

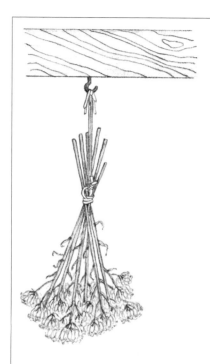

▲ FIGURE 1. Air dry a bunch of flowers by securing the stems with a rubber band through which you have looped a twist tie. Hang the bunch by the twist tie with a piece of string (*Method 1*).

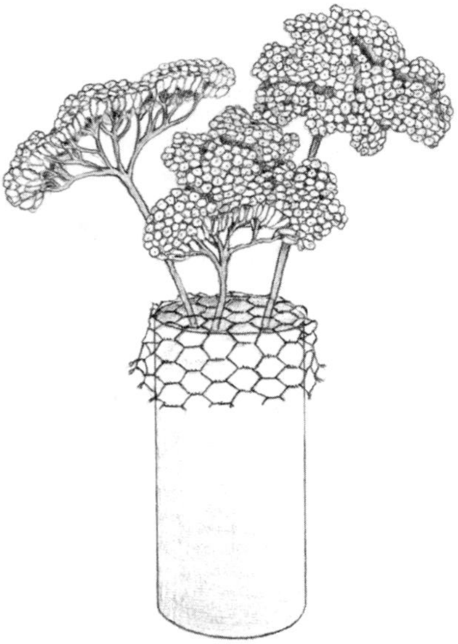

▲ FIGURE 2. Cover˙ the mouth of a 40-ounch juice can with a piece of chicken wire and, without crowding the heavy-headed flowers, insert stems through the holes (*Method 2*).

UPRIGHT, IN CONTAINERS WITH WATER
METHOD 3

If you are air drying baby's-breath (*Gypsophila paniculata*), bells-of-Ireland (*Moluccella laevis*), cockscomb (*Celosia cristata*), fern-leaf yarrow (*Achillea filipendulina*), any of the *Hydrangea* species, or mimosa (*Acacia dealbata*) in an upright position, it will also be necessary to put about an inch (2.5 cm) of water in the bottom of the container (Figure 3). These species would wilt without the addition of water and this method has been known to work when others have failed. Allow the water to evaporate, then dry the material as described in Method 2.

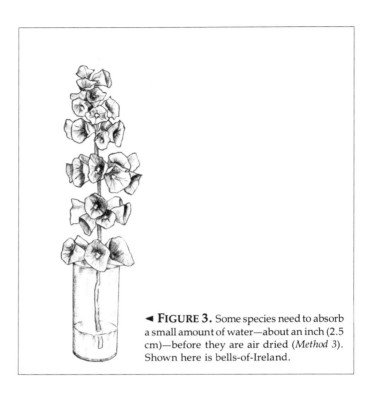

◄ **FIGURE 3.** Some species need to absorb a small amount of water—about an inch (2.5 cm)—before they are air dried (*Method 3*). Shown here is bells-of-Ireland.

UPRIGHT, IN OASIS
METHOD 4

Those who have done any flower arranging will be familiar with Oasis: a soft foam material into which flower stems can be pushed to hold them in position. It must be wetted before use. Oasis Sec is harder and used dry to hold everlastings and some of the lighter dried materials. It is also known by the trade name Sahara. Ultra Foam is harder still.

The different Oasis types come in a variety of colors—green, white, and brown being the most commonly used. A number of shapes and sizes are also obtainable.

For a one-step arrangement, you can put fresh flowers that air dry well, upright, into Oasis Sec (Sahara) or into Ultra Foam, and allow them to dry in situ.

AIR DRYING
WITH WARMTH OR FORCED AIR
METHODS 5–10

THE AIR DRYING of plants can be speeded up by providing a current of gently moving warm air. Temperatures under 120°F (50°C) are suitable. The length of time the material will take to dry will depend on the temperature and its succulence, but check it often until it has dried to your satisfaction. As with most drying procedures, trial and error combined with common sense are the best guides to follow.

AN ELECTRIC FOOD DEHYDRATOR
METHOD 5

An electric food dehydrator supplies a flow of air at a controlled temperature, which is ideal for drying many types of flowers. The shelves of the dehydrator are made of screens whose holes are usually 1/8 of an inch (3 mm) square or 1/6 of an inch (4 mm) square. To dry small flowers, the stems can be pushed through the mesh of the shelves to support the heads. They should be spaced far enough apart so that they do not touch.

It is difficult to give exact temperatures and times for drying, but any temperature between 100° and 120°F (40° and 50°C) may be needed. Drying time may take anywhere from six to eight hours. Much will depend, as usual, on the succulence of the material you have chosen for drying. So experiment with a few flowers before filling the dehydrator.

You can also use a desiccant (an artificial drying medium) in combination with the dehydrator. To do this remove the shelves. You will need a box that fits on the floor of the dehydrator and is about 4 inches (10 cm) deeper than the height of the tallest flower (excluding the stem) you want to dry. Such a depth is necessary to hold sufficient desiccant to support the flower heads and to absorb all the moisture being retained by the plant materials. See pages 96 to 99 for a more detailed description of how to dry with desiccants.

I am sure it is unnecessary to say don't use a solar dryer!

A COUNTERTOP CONVECTION OVEN
METHOD 6

A convection oven can be used in a manner similar to that of an electric food dehydrator. A convection oven is suitable for drying flowers only if the thermostat can be turned low enough to keep the temperature between 100° and 120°F (40° and 50°C). It can also be used if you can activate the fan without heat; this is possible in ovens used to defrost frozen food.

The heating element in a convection oven is smaller than that of a conventional electric oven, and a fan beside the element enables hot/warm air to circulate continuously. This continuous air flow, whether warm or cold, and a uniform oven temperature, ensures even drying of the flowers.

Although convection ovens can be used in a similar way to a food dehydrator, only some brands have dehydrating *accessories* available. These accessories consist of specially made screens or drying racks that fit in the shelf slots of the oven.

For drying flowers, however, it is easy to make your own. There are two alternatives. If you are going to use some warmth to dry your flowers buy some rug hooking canvas and cut it to fit over your shelves; get the kind with seven squares to the inch. If you are going to dry without heat, plastic net canvas is more rigid and easier to handle. This comes in pieces about 10 by 13 inches (25 by 32 cm). Either type of canvas can be spread on the oven shelves and the flower stems poked through the holes. Both types of canvas can be cut with scissors, both are washable, and they can be purchased at hobby and craft shops.

WARMTH NEAR A FURNACE
METHOD 7

It has been recommended that plant material can be hung over a furnace to dry—a practice of which I do not approve. You have no control over the amount of heat and could very well ruin your material. Certainly a dark, dry basement that has a furnace is a good place to hang plant material to dry, but do not put it directly over the source of the heat.

A CUPBOARD AROUND A HOT WATER TANK
METHOD 8

As a child in Britain, I remember almost every house had an "airing cupboard." Built around the hot water tank (usually in the bathroom), it had slatted shelves to store household linen. The other day I read that these cupboards are now being built in new residential construction in North America. Dark, dry, and warm, they are a perfect place to dry flowers. Large heads can be hung upside down from the shelves with a twist of florist's wire; smaller flowers can be dried by threading the stems through the slats.

A GAS OVEN WITH A PILOT LIGHT
METHOD 9

Another warm, dark place that can be used to dry flowers (and herbs) with steady warmth is a gas oven because it has a protected pilot light. You may use the regular oven racks covered with rug hooking canvas or plastic net canvas described in Method 6. Just be careful not to turn on the oven when it is full of plant material!

AN ELECTRIC OVEN
METHOD 10

I have never tried using an electric oven, so I cannot speak from experience. However, if you can dry herbs in your electric oven, I do not see why you cannot dry flowers. You must be able to maintain the oven temperature between 100° and 120°F (40° and 50°C). The exact temperature you use and the length of time it takes depends, as usual, on the succulence of what you are drying.

ð   ð   ð

All forms of air drying, whether with warmth or not, are simple and trouble free. Just remember:

ð Low humidity and good air circulation are crucial.

ð A little warmth is often needed.

ð Heat is seldom necessary. You don't want to dry your material to such a point that it becomes brittle and shatters when touched.

All the methods of drying and preserving (desiccants, preservatives, pressing) that follow are more time consuming than any form of air drying.

ð   ð   ð

Following are two lists of plants that air dry by one or more of the methods just described. The first list gives the common name of each plant in alphabetical order, followed by its Latin name, the recommended drying method, and drying tips. The second list is the reverse: the Latin name followed by the common name.

AIR-DRIED PLANT MATERIAL
SOME DOS & DON'TS

DO store material in warm, dry, dark place.

DON'T store where there isn't any warmth, and **DON'T** store them in a cupboard around a hot water tank (a good place to *dry* some things, but material stored there could become brittle).

DON'T store materials near any heat source: even greater fragility and brittleness will result.

DO store where the humidity is under 60 percent and preferably under 50 percent. A hygrometer is used to measure humidity; not to be confused with a hydrometer, which measures the specific gravity of liquids.

DON'T overcrowd the material in storage boxes.

DO leave space for air to circulate around and through hanging bunches.

DON'T store materials where the temperature fluctuates.

DON'T store dried plants in an outside shed, greenhouse, or damp garage.

DON'T use cardboard boxes for storage if the climate is humid.

DO separate and support the dried-plant material with crimpled tissue paper if it has to be stored two or more layers deep in its container.

DO store boxes where they won't have to be moved often.

DO store glass containers of material in a dark cupboard; **DON'T** store glass containers where any light can fall on them.

DO store scented and unscented material apart.

DON'T store material with *different* scents together.

DO remember that if you have no cover for a box, plastic food wrap can be used, but tape it securely to the box with a reusable tape, such as Scotch Magic Plus.

DO remember to put silica gel with dried-plant material stored in plastic bags, or condensation may form on the inside of the bag.

PLANTS THAT AIR DRY WELL
COMMON NAME/*LATIN NAME*

Common Name	Latin Name	M.N.*	Drying Tips
Ageratum	*Ageratum*	3	Blue & white flowers dry well
Bear's-breech	*Acanthus* spp	1, 2	Dry flowers and foliage
Bird-of-paradise	*Strelitzia reginae*	3	Dry flowers
Blanket flower	*Gaillardia aristata*	1	Dry flowers
Blazing-star	*Liatris spicata*	7, 8	Dry when flowers at top of spike are open
Blue lace flower	*Trachymene coerulea*	7, 8	Dry when flowers are fully open
Box, common	*Buxus sempervirens*	3	Dry foliage
Broom	*Cytisus* spp	1,7,8	Tie stems in curves while drying
Broom	*Genista* spp	1,7,8	Tie stems in curves while drying
Broom, Scotch	*Cytisus scoparius*	1,7,8	Best broom for holding curves
Candle larkspur	*Delphinium elatum*	1,7,8	Dry before lowest flower is open
Chrysanthemum	*Chrysanthemum* spp & var.	2,7,8	For pom-poms. Method 1 for small yellow or white flowers
Clary sage	*Salvia sclarea*	1	Dry flowers and foliage
Coneflower	*Rudbeckia* spp	1,2,4	Remove petals, dry centers
Cornflower; bachelor's-button	*Centaurea cyanus*	1	Wire, then dry buds & immature flowers
Dusty Miller	*Artemisia stellerana*	1	Foliage dries well
False dragonhead; obedience	*Physostegia virginiana*	1	Dry calyx-covered runners
False goat's-beard	*Astilbe biternata*	1	Dry when blooms open at base
Goldenrod	*Solidago* spp	1,7,8	Dry before flowers fully mature
Heath	*Erica* spp	1, 3	Dry before flowers fully mature
Heather	*Calluna* spp	1, 3	Dry before flowers fully mature
Hop, common	*Humulus lupulus*	1, 3	Dry foliage & flowers
Hydrangea	*Hydrangea paniculata*	3,7,8	Cut before frost when green or pinkish
Hydrangea, florist's; hydrangea, French	*Hydrangea macrophylla*	1, 2	Cut in fall after color changes
Lady's-mantle	*Alchemilla* spp	1,6,7	Cut flowers when mature
Lamb's-ears	*Stachys byzantina*	1,7,8	Dry the wooly foliage
Larkspur	*Consolida regalis*	1	Cut stems when flowers open
Lavender	*Lavandula* spp	1,7,8	Dry when all flowers on spike open

*M.N. = method number throughout

Common Name	Latin Name	M.N.*	Drying Tips
Lavender cotton	*Santolina chamaecyparissus*	1, 3	Silver foliage dries well
Mimosa	*Acacia dealbata*	1,7,8	Flowers dry well; remove foliage
Montebretia	*Crocosmia crocosmiiflora*	1,7,8	Flowers dry well
Oats	*Avena sativa*	2	Turns beige when dry
Onions; leeks; garlic; chives; etc.	*Allium* spp	1, 2	Leeks especially
Peony	*Paeonia* spp	1	Double white, pink, and red dry best
Pincushions	*Scabiosa atropurpurea*	1	Cut when petals have fallen
Plantain lily	*Hosta* spp	5,6,8	Dry foliage
Protea; king protea	*Protea cynaroides*	3	Dry white, red, bicolored
Pussy willow	*Salix caprea, S. discolor*	1,7,8	Cut before catkins are open
Queen-Anne's-lace	*Daucus carota*	1	Cut just before white flowers mature
Ravenna grass	*Erianthus ravennae*	1	Cut before seeds mature
Rocket larkspur	*Consolida ambigua*	1	Dry foliage and flower buds
Rosemary	*Rosmarinus officinalis*	1,7,8	Retains its fragrance when dried
Rue, common	*Ruta graveolens*	1, 2	Gray-green foliage retains scent
Rush	*Juncus* spp	1, 2	Cut sparingly in the wild
Sage, blue; mealy-cup sage	*Salvia farinacea*	1	Flowers and foliage dry well
Sedge	*Carex* spp	2	Cut sparingly in the wild
Silver-dollar gum	*Eucalyptus polyanthemos*	1	One of the many florist's varieties
Silver king artemisia	*Artemisia ludoviciana albula*	1	Dry foliage
Silver-leaved mountain gum	*Eucalyptus pulverulenta*	1	One of the many florist's varieties
Sweet corn; Indian corn	*Zea mays*	1	Dry leaves and tassels at all stages
Sweet-sultan	*Centaurea moschata*	1,7,8	Flowers are thistlelike and fragrant
Tansy, common	*Tanacetum vulgare*	1	Dry compact yellow flower heads
Wheat, common	*Triticum aestivum*	1, 2	Cut at different stages of development
Zinnia	*Zinnia* spp	3	Dry mature yellow, green, and white flowers

PLANTS THAT AIR DRY WELL

LATIN NAME/COMMON NAME

Latin Name	Common Name	Latin Name	Common Name
Acacia dealbata	Mimosa	*Gaillardia aristata*	Blanket flower
Acanthus spp	Bear's-breech	*Hosta* spp	Plantain lily
Ageratum	Ageratum	*Humulus lupulus*	Hop, common
Alchemilla spp	Lady's-mantle	*Hydrangea macrophylla*	Hydrangea, florist's; hydrangea, French
Allium spp	Onion; leeks; garlic; chives; etc.		
Artemisia ludoviciana albula	Silver king artemisia	*Hydrangea paniculata*	Hydrangea
		Juncus spp	Rush
Artemisia stellerana	Dusty Miller	*Lavandula* spp	Lavender
Astilbe biternata	False goat's-beard	*Liatris spicata*	Blazing-star
Avena sativa	Oats	*Paeonia* spp	Peony
Buxus sempervirens	Box, common	*Physostegia virginiana*	False dragonhead; obedience
Calluna spp	Heather		
Carex spp	Sedge	*Protea cynaroides*	Protea; king protea
Centaurea cyanus	Cornflower; bachelor's-button	*Rosmarinus officinalis*	Rosemary
		Rudbeckia spp	Coneflower
Centurea moschata	Sweet-sultan	*Ruta graveolens*	Rue, common
Chrysanthemum spp & var.	Chrysanthemum	*Salix caprea, S. discolor*	Pussy willow
Consolida ambigua	Rocket larkspur	*Salvia farinacea*	Sage, blue; mealy-cup sage
Consolida regalis	Larkspur		
Crocosmia crocosmiiflora	Montebretia	*Salvia sclarea*	Clary sage
Cytisus spp	Broom	*Santolina chamaecyparissus*	Lavender cotton
Cytisus scoparius	Broom, Scotch	*Scabiosa atropurpurea*	Pincushions
Daucus carota	Queen-Anne's-lace	*Solidago* spp	Goldenrod
		Stachys byzantina	Lamb's-ears
Delphinium elatum	Candle larkspur	*Strelitzia reginae*	Bird-of-paradise
Erianthus ravennae	Ravenna grass	*Tanacetum vulgare*	Tansy, common
Erica spp	Heath	*Trachymene coerulea*	Blue lace flower
Eucalyptus polyanthemos	Silver-dollar gum	*Triticum aestivum*	Wheat, common
Eucalyptus pulverulenta	Silver-leaved mountain gum	*Zea mays*	Sweet corn; Indian corn
Genista spp	Broom	*Zinnia* spp	Zinnia

PLANTS THAT AIR DRY WELL

1. Bird-of-paradise (*Strelitzia reginae*)
2. Scotch Broom (*Cytisus scoparius*)
3. Blue lace flower (*Trachymene coerulea*)
4. Cornflower (*Centaurea cyanus*)
5. Bear's-breech (*Acanthus mollis*)
6. Chives (*Allium schoenoprasum*)
7. Oats (*Avena sativa*)

DRYING
WITH DESICCANTS

METHODS 11 & 12

FLOWERS THAT DO NOT DRY WELL by any air-drying method can often be preserved by using a desiccant. Even those plants that can be air dried quite successfully will retain a more natural color when a desiccant is used, and almost any flower will retain its shape better (especially trumpet- and cup-shaped ones) than if it were air dried.

But a lot of time and patience are needed when using any desiccant because it is a procedure which needs meticulous care.

You will need boxes of various sizes with well-fitting lids, or one that can be covered with plastic wrap to make an airtight seal. Cardboard, plastic, or wooden boxes will all serve the purpose. If you want to dry tall spikes on their own stems, cylinder-shaped containers or a long narrow box will be necessary. You will also need various thicknesses of floral wire (17-gauge for heavy material, 20-gauge for medium-weight stems, and 28-gauge for very fine stems), and your chosen desiccant—all of which should be available at craft shops.

GENERAL PROCEDURES

Be sure that the flowers you pick for preserving with any desiccant are in perfect condition. If possible, they should have just opened—this is when they are most sturdy. Another requirement is that they should be picked when they are quite dry after several hours (or preferably days) of sunshine. It would be ideal to put them straight into the chosen desiccant. However, if you have to hold them awhile, put the stems of heavy material into a container of warm water; smaller flowers can be held in wet Oasis. Be sure to dry or cut off any wet part of the stems before putting them into a desiccant and strip off all the foliage.

It is important to give the drying flowers plenty of room in the desiccant. Be sure there is space between each flower head and that the petals from different flowers do not touch.

Some flowers should be dried face up. Leave a short stem of about 2 inches (5 cm), push half its length into a piece of Styrofoam cut to fit the bottom of the drying box, and then carefully trickle your chosen desiccant onto the Styrofoam (about an inch deep) and into and around the petals until the flower is quite covered and filled. Or you could wire the stem, bend it into a right angle below the flower head, place it in a box or container, and then cover the flower with desiccant (Figure 4). This method is effective for drying daffodils, tulips, crocus, and any other trumpet- or cup-shaped flowers. It is also the best way to dry the heavy, many-petaled flowers, such as African marigolds, roses, peonies, and double dahlias. For other flowers that dry well by this method, see the lists that begin on page 103.

To dry flowers face down, the stems should again be cut about 2 inches (5 cm) long. Add the desiccant to a depth of 2 inches (5 cm) in the bottom of the box, and create a little mound on which to place each flower (Figure 5). Put a single flower on each mound, then trickle

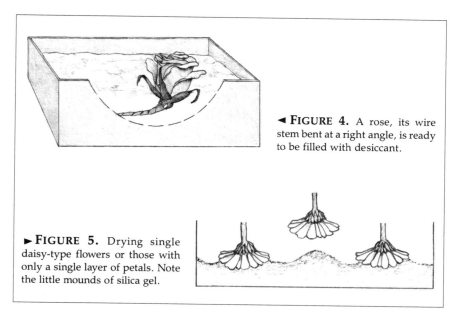

◄ **FIGURE 4.** A rose, its wire stem bent at a right angle, is ready to be filled with desiccant.

► **FIGURE 5.** Drying single daisy-type flowers or those with only a single layer of petals. Note the little mounds of silica gel.

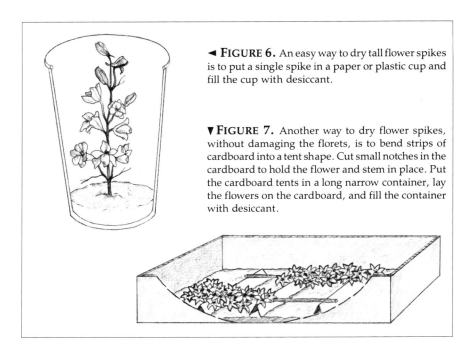

◄ **FIGURE 6.** An easy way to dry tall flower spikes is to put a single spike in a paper or plastic cup and fill the cup with desiccant.

▼ **FIGURE 7.** Another way to dry flower spikes, without damaging the florets, is to bend strips of cardboard into a tent shape. Cut small notches in the cardboard to hold the flower and stem in place. Put the cardboard tents in a long narrow container, lay the flowers on the cardboard, and fill the container with desiccant.

the desiccant over the back of the flower until it is buried. This method is good for drying all kinds of single, daisy-type flowers and ones with only a single layer of petals.

Use the little 2-inch (5-cm) stems to handle the flowers at all times.

To dry tall spikes of flowers you will need either a cylinder tall enough to hold the spike upright or a long box (Figures 6 and 7). In either case, the flower spike must be completely encased in the desiccant. Some of the flowers that can be dried this way are gladioli, delphiniums, and hollyhocks, but a lot of desiccant will be required. The alternative is to remove the blossoms, then dry and use them individually. You can, if you have the patience and manual dexterity, wire them on to a stem once they have dried!

When you are checking to see if the flowers are dry, be very gentle. Tip the container until some of the petals are exposed and feel them. If they are still soft they need more time in the desiccant. If they feel like dry tissue paper they are ready. If they are brittle and crumble they have been in too long and will be a total loss!

If you are using cardboard boxes it is a good idea to punch small holes in the bottom of them before putting in any desiccant. Cover these holes with masking tape. Then when you need to get rid of the desiccant, remove the tape and let it trickle out—care and patience are absolutely necessary to avoid any damage to the delicate dried flowers. If you have pushed your upward facing flowers into Styrofoam you will need to cut a channel in the Styrofoam directly over a box hole to allow the desiccant to run out.

So that all of the flowers in a box are dry at the same time do not mix many-petaled flowers with single-petaled ones. It is difficult to give the exact times that any specific flower must remain in a desiccant. This will depend on the amount of moisture in the tissues of the material being dried and the desiccant being used. It can vary from two or three days to as much as three weeks—just check the material regularly until it is quite dry.

When you take the flowers out some of the desiccant may stick to the petals. To remove it, hold the flower upside down by its stem and tap or flick the stem with your finger. Any desiccant that still sticks to the petals should be gently brushed off with a soft camel-hair brush, such as an artist's paintbrush or a photographer's lens brush. In a humid atmosphere the dried material will reabsorb moisture readily, so once you have gone to the trouble to dry plant material, keep it dry with proper storage (see pages 195 to 198).

SILICA GEL
METHOD 11

Flowers dried with silica gel retain their color better than those dried by any other method, and they dry faster. Silica gel can be bought as rough crystals, fine crystals, and in a sandy form. It is not a jelly-like substance as its name would imply. Tiny packets of silica gel crystals are occasionally found inside bottles of medication in order to keep it dry. These can be used again when storing dried flowers, but it is the fine ground, sandy form that you will need for use as a desiccant.

Silica gel is available at hobby and craft shops, some florists, chemical supply houses, garden shops, and at some hardware and drugstores. Sometimes it is sold under a trade name, such as Flower-Dri. It is not cheap, so shop around and buy it in bulk if you can. You will probably need at least 5 pounds. It will last forever, so the initial investment will be justified if you intend to dry many flowers.

Silica gel is not toxic, but avoid inhaling it because it can irritate your sinuses (you might want to wear a mask over your nose and mouth). It can absorb almost half its own weight in water and still feel powdery, but remember that however powdery it feels, if it is white or even pale pink in color it needs drying. You can reactivate its desiccative properties by heating it in the oven, well spread out in a shallow container, for 20 to 30 minutes at a temperature of 250°F (120°C). In a microwave oven it will take about 2 minutes on high. When it is blue it's ready to use again. When not in use, silica gel must be kept in an absolutely airtight container or it will absorb moisture from the air. *Cool* it in an airtight container with the lid tightly secured.

To use silica gel for drying flowers follow the general instructions on the use of desiccants, pages 96 to 99. Flowers will take from 48 hours to 5 or 6 days to dry in silica gel. The exact length of time depends principally on the moisture content of the material being dried.

However, if you are in a hurry, you can speed up the process by using the silica gel when it is still warm from the oven. Extra care must be taken to see that the flowers are not left too long in the warm silica gel or they will become brittle. Two other fast preserving/drying techniques are pressing with silica gel (Method 18) and drying flowers in silica gel in a microwave (Method 13).

Foliage of the following plants will dry well in silica gel: rosemary, rhododendron, lily-of-the-valley, bear's-breech.

SAND, BORAX, AND CORNMEAL
METHOD 12

Sand must be clean. Buy a grade of washed fine sand because its purity can be assured better than sand gathered at the beach. Because it is so heavy, it is only suitable to use by itself for a few heavy-petaled flowers, such as peonies and large-flowered dahlias. It can be used for more delicate flowers in combination with other desiccants. The proportion *must* be 1 cup of sand to 2 cups of borax *or* cornmeal *or* silica gel. Plant material may take as long as three weeks to dry using sand and sand mixes. Pom-pom dahlias dry well this way.

If you cannot buy clean, washed sand it will be necessary to sterilize whatever sand you intend to use. To do this, spread a thin layer of sand on a shallow baking pan, and put it in the oven at 250°F

(120 °C). So that you may know when it is absolutely dry, mix a little silica gel in with the sand. As soon as the silica gel turns blue the sand will be sterile and dry. Cool the sand before using it.

Borax used by itself has several disadvantages. Delicate flowers left in it just a few hours too long will develop burn spots on their petals. It also tends to cake as soon as it gets the slightest bit damp (after absorbing moisture from the flowers). So use it in a mix, either with sand as described above, or in a proportion of 1 cup of borax to 1 cup cornmeal. The latter mix (borax and cornmeal) is particularly good for delicate plant material because it is lightweight. Larkspur dries well this way when at least half of the florets have opened.

Depending on what type of material is being dried, borax and borax mixes will take from 48 hours to seven or eight days to work. As mentioned above, be sure to brush off any desiccant that contains borax as soon as the flowers are dry to prevent burn spots.

Cornmeal should never be used alone because weevils like it and they'll make a feast of your plant material! If you need a light desiccant, use it (as mentioned above) with borax.

PLANT MATERIAL DRIED IN ANY DESICCANT
SOME DOS & DON'TS

DO make all storage boxes and tins airtight.
DO use waterproof tape to seal all storage containers.
DO take special care of flowers that have been dried in silica gel: they will be brittle and reabsorb moisture very easily.

&❧& &❧& &❧&

Following are two lists of flowers that dry well in silica gel. The first list gives the common name in alphabetical order followed by the Latin name, how to place the flowers in the desiccant, and occasional method recommendations. The second list gives the Latin name alphabetically, followed by the common name.

Many of the flowers on the lists that follow will also dry in other desiccants (Method 12), but silica gel gives much superior results and I feel that in spite of the initial expense, it's worth it in the long run. All of the flowers listed will dry in cold or warm silica gel (Method 11) and in silica gel heated by a microwave oven (Method 13).

FLOWERS THAT DRY WELL IN SILICA GEL

1. Wallflower (*Cheiranthus cheiri*)
2. Sweet violet (*Viola odorata*)
3. Geranium (*Pelargonium zonale*)
4. English primrose (*Primula vulgaris*)
5. Pot marigold (*Calendula officinalis*)
6. Stemless gentian (*Gentiana acaulis*)
7. Christmas rose (*Helleborus niger*)
8. California poppy (*Eschscholzia californica*)

1. Gladiola, corn flag (*Gladiolus* x *gandavensis*)
2. Lily-of-the-valley (*Convallaria majalis*)
3. Dutch crocus (*Crocus vernus*)
4. Bells-of-Ireland (*Moluccella laevis*)
5. Columbine (*Aquilegia* spp)
6. Common buttercup (*Ranunculus acris*)
7. Poet's narcissus (*Narcissus poeticus*)
8. Daffodil (*Narcissus*)

FLOWERS THAT DRY WELL IN SILICA GEL
COMMON NAME/*LATIN NAME*

Common Name	Latin Name	Placement; Method No.
Aster	*Callistephus* spp	Face down
Azalea	*Rhododendron* spp	Dry individual florets face up
Bells-of-Ireland	*Moluccella laevis*	Individual calyxes should be face up
Bird-of-paradise	*Strelitzia reginae*	Dry individual florets or give stem support
Bleeding-heart	*Dicentra spectabilis*	Face up
Blue lace flower	*Trachymene coerulea*	Face down
Blue sage	*Salvia azurea*	Dry whole spikes upright
Buttercup, common	*Ranunculus acris*	Buds upright, open flowers face down
Buttercup, double	*Ranunculus acris* 'Flore Pleno'	Face up
Butterfly bush	*Buddleia davidii*	Lay horizontal, supported
Camellia, common	*Camellia japonica*	Face up
Candytuft	*Iberis* spp	Face up
Canterbury-bells	*Campanula medium*	Face up
Carnation	*Dianthus caryophyllus*	Dry before fully open, face up
Chamomile	*Chamaemelum nobile*	Face down
Christmas rose	*Helleborus niger*	Face up
Chrysanthemum	*Chrysanthemum* spp & var.	Singles face down, doubles face up
Clary sage	*Salvia sclarea*	Face up
Clematis	*Clematis* spp	Face up
Columbine	*Aquilegia* spp	Face up
Coneflower	*Rudbeckia* spp	Face down
Cornflower; bachelor's-button	*Centaurea cyanus*	Face down
Crocus	*Crocus* spp	Face up; Method 13
Cup-and-saucer vine; Mexican ivy	*Cobaea scandens*	Face up
Daffodil	*Narcissus* spp & var.	Face up; Method 13
Dahlia, annual and perennial	*Dahlia* spp & var.	Doubles face up, singles face down
Daisy, African	*Lonas annua*	Face down; Method 13

☞

Common Name	Latin Name	Placement; Method No.
Daisy, English	*Bellis perennis*	Face down; Method 13
Daisy, gloriosa	*Rudbeckia hirta gloriosa*	Face down; Method 13
Daisy, Paris; Margeurite	*Chrysanthemum frutescens*	Face down; Method 13
Daisy, shasta	*Chrysanthemum maximum* (and *C.* x *superbum*)	Face down; Method 13
Daisy, Transvaal	*Gerbera jamesonii*	Face down; Method 13
Delphinium	*Delphinium* spp & var.	Dry individual florets
Dogwood	*Cornus* spp	Face up; Method 13 (A protected plant and illegal to pick in the wild)
Edelweiss	*Leontopodium alpinum*	Face up
Feverfew	*Chrysanthemum parthenium*	Face down
Forget-me-not, garden	*Myosotis sylvatica*	Face down
Forsythia; golden-bells	*Forsythia* spp	Dry short sprays horizontally
Foxglove	*Digitalis* spp	Dry individual florets face up
Freesia	*Freesia* spp	Dry individual florets face up
Fuchsia	*Fuchsia* spp & var.	Face up
Gentian	*Gentiana* spp	Face up
Gentian sage	*Salvia patens*	Dry individual spikes, supported
Geranium	*Pelargonium* spp & var.	Dry individual florets face up
Gladiolus	*Gladiolus* spp	Dry individual florets face up
Globe thistle, small	*Echinops ritro*	Face up
Grape hyacinth	*Muscari botryoides*	Upright; Method 13
Heath	*Erica* spp	Dry upright or horizontal
Heather	*Calluna* spp	Dry upright or horizontal
Hollyhock	*Alcea rosea*	Single flowers face down, double flowers face up
Hyacinth, common	*Hyacinthus orientalis*	Dry individual florets face up
Hydrangea	*Hydrangea paniculata*	Whole heads supported or florets laid flat
Larkspur	*Consolida regalis*	Dry individual florets with the cups facing up
Lavender	*Lavandula* spp	Lay flat

Common Name	Latin Name	Placement; Method No.
Lavender cotton	*Santolina chamaecyparissus*	Face down
Lily	*Lilium* spp & var.	Face up
Lily, African	*Agapanthus africanus*	Face up with support
Lily-of-the-valley	*Convallaria majalis*	Lay flat; Method 13
Love-in-a-mist	*Nigella damascena*	Face down
Marigold	*Tagetes* spp	Face up; Method 13
Marigold, pot	*Calendula officinalis*	Face down
Margeurite; daisy, Paris	*Chrysanthemum frutescens*	Face down
Marsh malllow	*Althaea officinalis*	Face down
Mimosa	*Acacia dealbata*	Dry individual florets; Method 13
Mock orange	*Philadelphus coronarius*	Face down
Mexican sunflower	*Tithonia rotundifolia*	Face down
Pansy; violet	*Viola* spp	Face up; Method 13
Pasque flower	*Anemone pulsatilla*	Face up
Peony	*Paeonia* spp	Face up
Phlox	*Phlox* spp	Dry individual florets face up
Pincushions	*Scabiosa atropurpurea*	Face up
Pinks	*Dianthus* spp	Singles face down, doubles face up
Poppy	*Papaver* spp & var.	Most face up; Method 13
Primrose, English	*Primula vulgaris*	Face down
Queen-Anne's-lace	*Daucus carota*	Face down
Rhododendron	*Rhododendron* spp & var.	Dry individual florets face up
Rose	*Rosa* spp & var.	Face up; Method 13 best
Snow-on-the-mountain	*Euphorbia marginata*	Face down
Stock, evening	*Matthiola longipetala*	Face down; retains scent
Sunflower, common	*Helianthus annuus*	Face up
Tickseed	*Coreopsis* spp	Face down
Tulip	*Tulipa* spp & var.	Face up; Method 13
Verbena, garden	*Verbena* x *hybrida*	Dry individual florets face down
Veronica; speedwell	*Veronica* spp	Face up
Violet, sweet	*Viola odorata*	Face down

☞

Common Name	Latin Name	Placement; Method No.
Water lily, European white	*Nymphaea alba*	Face up; A protected species and illegal to pick in the wild
Windflower	*Anemone* spp	Face up; Method 13
Yarrow	*Achillea* spp	Face down
Zinnia	*Zinnia* spp	Face up; Method 13

FLOWERS THAT DRY WELL IN SILICA GEL
LATIN NAME/COMMON NAME

Latin Name	Common Name	Latin Name	Common Name
Acacia dealbata	Mimosa	*Clematis*	Clematis
Achillea spp	Yarrow	*Cobaea scandens*	Cup-and-saucer vine; Mexican ivy
Agapanthus africanus	Lily, African		
Althaea officinalis	Marsh mallow	*Consolida regalis*	Larkspur
Alcea rosea	Hollyhock	*Convallaria majalis*	Lily-of-the-valley
Anemone spp	Windflower	*Coreopsis* spp	Tickseed
Anemone pulsatilla	Pasque flower	*Cornus* spp	Dogwood
Aquilegia spp	Columbine	*Crocus* spp	Crocus
Bellis perennis	Daisy, English	*Dahlia* spp & var.	Dahlia, annual and perennial
Buddleia davidii	Butterfly bush		
Calendula officinalis	Marigold, pot	*Daucus carota*	Queen-Anne's-lace
Callistephus spp	Aster		
Calluna spp	Heather	*Delphinium* spp & var.	Delphinium
Camellia japonica	Camellia, common	*Dianthus* spp	Pinks
Campanula medium	Canterbury-bells	*Dianthus caryophyllus*	Carnation
Centaurea cyanus	Cornflower; bachelor's-button	*Dicentra spectabilis*	Bleeding-heart
		Digitalis spp	Foxglove
Chamaemelum nobile	Chamomile	*Echinops ritro*	Globe thistle, small
Chrysanthemum spp & var.	Chrysanthemum	*Erica* spp	Heath
Chrysanthemum frutescens	Daisy, Paris; Margeurite	*Euphorbia marginata*	Snow-on-the-mountain
Chrysanthemum maximum (and *C.* x *superbum*)	Daisy, shasta	*Forsythia* spp	Forsythia; golden-bells
Chrysanthemum parthenium	Feverfew	*Freesia* spp	Freesia

Latin Name	Common Name	Latin Name	Common Name
Fuchsia spp & var.	Fuchsia	*Phlox* spp	Phlox
Gentiana spp	Gentian	*Primula vulgaris*	Primrose, English
Gerbera jamesonii	Daisy, Transvaal	*Ranunculus acris*	Buttercup, common
Gladiolus spp	Gladiolus		
Helianthus annuus	Sunflower, common	*Ranunculus acris* 'Flore Pleno'	Buttercup, double
Helleborus niger	Christmas rose	*Rhododendron* spp & var.	Azalea
Hyacinthus orientalis	Hyacinth, common	*Rhododendron* spp & var.	Rhododendron
		Rosa spp & var.	Rose
Hydrangea paniculata	Hydrangea	*Rudbeckia* spp	Coneflower
Iberis spp	Candytuft	*Rudbeckia hirta gloriosa*	Daisy, gloriosa
Lavandula spp	Lavender	*Salvia azurea*	Blue sage
Lilium spp & var.	Lily	*Salvia patens*	Gentian sage
Leontopodium alpinum	Edelweiss	*Salvia sclarea*	Clary sage
Lonus annua	Daisy, African	*Santolina chamaecyparissus*	Lavender cotton
Matthiola longipetala	Stock, evening	*Scabiosa atropurpurea*	Pincushions
Moluccella laevis	Bells-of-Ireland	*Strelitzia reginae*	Bird-of-paradise
Muscari botryoides	Grape hyacinth	*Tagetes* spp	Marigold
Myosotis sylvatica	Forget-me-not, garden	*Tithonia rotundifolia*	Mexican sunflower
Narcissus spp	Daffodil	*Trachymene coerulea*	Blue lace flower
Nigella damascena	Love-in-a-mist	*Tulipa* spp & var.	Tulip
Nymphaea alba	Water lily, European white	*Verbena* x *hybrida*	Verbena, garden
		Veronica spp	Veronica; speedwell
Paeonia spp	Peony		
Papaver spp & var.	Poppy	*Viola* spp	Pansy; violet
Pelargonium spp & var.	Geranium	*Viola odorata*	Violet, sweet
Philadelphus coronarius	Mock orange	*Zinnia* spp	Zinnia

DRYING FLOWERS & LEAVES IN A MICROWAVE

METHODS 13 & 14

A MICROWAVE OVEN is a wonderful tool for drying plant material. It will retain the color and shape of flowers better than any other method. You can dry individual blossoms as they reach their peak drying condition, or leaves just as they turn the exact color you want. Instead of having materials drying for days or even weeks, you can harvest, preserve, and use them any way you wish in a matter of an hour or so.

Only dry one flower at a time—this will prevent crowding and over-drying, both of which could give undesirable results. This minimizes the time it has to be in the oven and ensures little or no loss of color and form. Keep records of all your trials and errors.

If you spoil a flower by this method because of some error in timing, or because the condition of the leaf was not quite right, you will have lost only the one specimen. If some variety that you particularly want to dry does not seem to do well, it may be because the moisture content of the flower was too low. Try again with blossoms at different stages of development. You can afford to experiment when drying with a microwave.

Any container suitable for food preparation in a microwave oven can be used to hold flowers: deep cups and mugs, small ovenproof glass bowls, measuring cups of glass or plastic. Leaves can be laid between the folds of a paper napkin; see the instructions for Method 14 for more on this procedure.

DRYING FLOWERS WITH SILICA GEL IN A MICROWAVE
METHOD 13

The procedure goes like this.

1) Pick only a few flowers to preserve in the microwave at a time.
2) Put some silica gel in a container in the oven for 1 minute on high until it is bright blue. The amount of silica gel is not crucial, but if you want a guide, a depth of 2 inches should do the trick.
3) Select a container of suitable size for the flower you want to dry.
4) Put 1 inch (2.5 cm) of silica gel in the bottom of the container and position the flower on it: face down for daisy-type flowers, face up for cup-shaped flowers (see pages 96 to 99 for more on how to position flowers in a desiccant).
5) Gently cover the flower with more silica gel. Put the container into the microwave oven on high for 1 minute.
6) Remove it and let it cool on the counter for 30 minutes.
7) Check to see if the flower is dry. If it is not, return the container to the oven for 1 more minute.
8) Remove it again and allow it to cool on the counter for another 30 minutes.
9) Containers that have been used in the microwave with silica gel **should not** be used later for food preparation.

If you have a microwave oven with a rotating rack, by all means use it to avoid any problem with uneven drying. If you do not have one, you may have to manually rotate the container halfway through the cycle to obtain evenly dried material.

DRYING LEAVES IN A MICROWAVE
METHOD 14

All you need to dry leaves in a microwave oven are some paper napkins. They should be the soft absorbent ones that are folded square to create four thicknesses. Follow these directions.

1) Open a napkin once; it will now have two thicknesses.
2) Put a few small leaves or one large leaf on one-half of the paper napkin and fold the other half over. The leaves must be entirely covered by the napkin.

3) Place a microwaveable mug or small plate (Corelle or other microwave safe brand) on top of the napkin and leaf "sandwich." This will prevent the leaf or leaves from curling.
4) Dry on high for 2 minutes.
5) Remove from the microwave and let it stand on the counter for about 20 minutes.
6) If the leaf is still moist it may need another minute in the oven.

Experiment with different kinds and conditions of leaves and adjust drying times until you achieve the desired results. Camellia, dogwood, lily-of-the-valley, ivy, hosta, and strawberry leaves all dry well by this method, as do many ferns. Also try drying any fall-tinted leaves you want to preserve in this manner.

GLYCERINE

METHOD 15

GLYCERINE IS EXCELLENT for preserving whole branches of mature foliage or individual leaves, but with a few exceptions is not suitable for preserving flowers (see lists on pages 117 to 118). It's an easy procedure and well worthwhile because the material preserved this way will last indefinitely. Mature leaves take on beautiful colors (both new colors and enhanced natural colors) and stay even more pliable than when alive on the branch (much like soft leather) and do not crack or break as easily.

PRESERVING WITH GLYCERINE
METHOD 15

You can buy glycerine from pharmacies, but it is expensive. It will be cheaper to buy it in bulk from a chemical supply company. Some people use antifreeze instead of glycerine and get interesting results. Not all foliage will absorb it, and even if it does, the colorant in the antifreeze can affect the color of the final product. But if you want to try it, test some on a small number of plants before doing large quantities of foliage.

A solution is usually made in a proportion by volume of one part glycerine to two parts water (i.e., 1 cup of glycerine to 2 cups of water). A professional florist told me that mixing half and half gave better results, but for large amounts of foliage this would be expensive. Whatever proportions you use mix the glycerine with *very hot, even boiling, water*, which will enable you to mix the two liquids thoroughly. The mixture can be used quite hot for woody stems, but should be cooled to room temperature for less tough material and for preserving individual leaves.

Foliage preserved in glycerine can be used in fresh or dried arrangements, Christmas wreaths, or swags. It combines well with fresh fruit for a table centerpiece.

HOW TO PRESERVE WHOLE BRANCHES OF FOLIAGE

Late summer and very early fall are the best seasons to gather most kinds of foliage for preserving in glycerine. The sap must still be rising so that the glycerine will be drawn up through the stems into the leaves to replace the water in the plant tissue. After two or three sunny days, cut the branches or stems of mature foliage in midmorning or early afternoon. This will ensure that all the material you wish to preserve is absolutely dry.

Main branches or stems should not be longer than 24 inches (60 cm). Cut side branches back to 12 to 14 inches (30 to 35 cm) in length—the glycerine solution would be unable to reach the leaves at the end of longer branches. If you find some of the leaves at the tips of the stems are drying out, wipe them over with some of the solution (not much is needed).

If there is bark on the branches or stems, scrape off about 4 inches (10 cm) at the base and either split them or crush them with a hammer. If there is no bark, strip the leaves from the bottom 4 inches (10 cm) of the stems.

If the leaves have drooped by the time they're ready for the glycerine solution, put the stems first into a container with 2 inches (5 cm) of warm water; if the leaves have not begun to "plump up" in about 12 hours, put the stems into 2 inches (5 cm) of boiling water until they do become turgid, an indication that they are absorbing the water. Fresh-cut branches that are not drooping can be put straight into the glycerine solution.

Choose a container just wide enough to hold upright the foliage you wish to preserve, pour in about 2 inches (5 cm) of a glycerine/water solution, and stand the plant material in it. The container of branches and glycerine solution will probably be top heavy, so put the whole thing into another large container weighed down with sand or pebbles to give it support, and put it in a cool dark place.

Leave the material in the solution for several days, checking each day to be sure that it has not all been absorbed. If it has, add a little more. After a few days you will know if the solution is being absorbed because the veins in the leaves will darken, the leaves themselves will feel soft and oily, and their color will have changed right to the tips. Green foliage may change to warm fall colors: red, brown, yellow, or bronze. The color change depends not only on the species being treated, but also the time of year when the foliage was gathered. Foliage that is naturally bronze or red changes very little when treated.

The branches should be removed from the solution when they attain the characteristics described above. If the solution is not being absorbed the underside of the leaves will start to ooze an oily liquid. If this happens, wipe it off with a soft tissue. It may be necessary to hang the whole branch upside down if the leaves are oozing, but you can see that the solution hasn't reached to the tips of the leaves. This is most often necessary *only* for those plants with very thick leaves.

If any leaves start to wilt while their stems are in the glycerine solution, it is because they are not absorbing the liquid. Cut the stems another inch or two, mash the ends, and put them back into the glycerine solution. If the solution seems too thick add a little water to thin it. Be sure to stir it well.

Your material will need anywhere from four days to four weeks, even more, in a glycerine solution. Soft-stemmed plants, such as dock (*Rumex* spp) and ivy (*Hedera* spp and var.), need less time in the solution than hard-stemmed plants, such as rosemary (*Rosmarinus officinalis*) or willow (*Salix* spp).

The glycerine solution can be used over and over again even if it turns brown and dirty looking. If mildew forms on top skim it off—the solution is still usable.

Plant material preserved in glycerine can be used in fresh or dried arrangements. But if you want to put the preserved branches in water with fresh-cut flowers, first dip the bottom 2 or 3 inches of the stem (5 to 7 cm) into melted paraffin wax. This will keep the stems dry and help to preserve them longer. If the leaves get dusty swish them gently in a weak solution of mild detergent, then dry them thoroughly with soft tissues.

HOW TO PRESERVE INDIVIDUAL LEAVES

Choose dry, thick, fully mature leaves, such as *Magnolia* (spp) and common camellia (*Camellia japonica*). Immature and thin leaves will probably go soft when soaked in a glycerine solution.

You will need:

- A long, fairly deep container (about the size of one used for making meat loaf) that you can cover securely with foil or plastic wrap.

🌹 Enough of the glycerine solution (1:2, glycerine to water as before) to put about 3 inches (7.5 cm) in the container.

🌹 A place to put the container where you won't upset it, but where you will see it and remember to look at it daily.

Put the leaves into the glycerine solution one at a time, making sure that each one is well covered. Don't crowd them—they must be able to float freely.

Every day *gently* slosh the solution about in the container by tipping it backwards and forwards. You must be sure that the leaves are kept covered by the solution and are not sticking to each other.

During the first few days the leaves may not take up the solution evenly and spots will appear. Don't worry—with time the solution will be absorbed evenly, the spots will disappear, and the leaves will become evenly colored throughout.

The leaves will need from one to three weeks immersed in the solution. It depends on how thick they are and how dry they were when picked. To dry them put the leaves on a thick pad of newspaper, cover with more newspapers, and leave them for about a week to ten days. At the end of this time there may be oily drops on the leaves. If so, wipe them off with soft tissues.

Leaf stems can be lengthened with wire (see pages 154 to 155 on Wiring).

HOW TO PRESERVE STRANDS OF IVY

Here is a tip given to me by a friend, which she has used successfully, though I have yet to try it.

You will need a pan to soak the ivy that is large enough to hold the strand you wish to preserve and enough glycerine solution to keep the ivy well covered. Leave it in the pan for four or five days, then remove it from the solution and wash it in tepid water. The ivy will remain green. Hang it up to drip, then lay it between a section of newspaper to dry. It will be interesting to see what color variegated ivy leaves turn.

BLEACHING PLANT MATERIAL

Sunlight can damage the color of drying or dried plant material. However, if you *want* to bleach foliage, flowers, grasses, or grains, hang them up in bright sunlight for a few weeks in a greenhouse or a very sunny window. Material being preserved in glycerine can be stood in the sun to make it fade.

You can soak seed heads and leaves in a solution of half household bleach (chlorine) and half water. They will need careful watching—if left too long in such a solution they will disintegrate.

GRASSES AND GRAINS THAT CAN BE PRESERVED

Any of the grasses, except Job's-tears (*Coix lacryma-jobi*), described in the first section of this book can be preserved in a glycerine solution. Their stems will be more supple than air-dried grasses. The same applies to grains such as oats, barley, millet, and wheat, which will turn a golden color after treatment with the glycerine. If you want the grain stems to stay green, pick them before the seed heads ripen, and hang them to dry; *don't* use glycerine to preserve them.

SOME FLOWERS THAT CAN BE PRESERVED IN GLYCERINE

As I mentioned before, baby's-breath (*Gypsophila paniculata*) is brittle and difficult to handle when dried, so any preservation procedure that does not make it brittle is well worth the trouble. Buy it fresh from the florist or cut it from your garden. The stems should be about 6 inches (15 cm) long. Stand it in the usual solution of glycerine for a few days, then hang it upside down to dry. You should be aware that this treatment will turn the flowers a creamy color.

The calyxes of bells-of-Ireland (*Moluccella laevis*) preserve well by total immersion in glycerine solution. Two or three days should be sufficient.

Seed heads and seedpods, many of which become brittle when dry, can be preserved in glycerine. Cut them with the required length of stem and put them in the standard solution and leave them for 24 to 48 hours. Chinese-lantern plant (*Physalis alkekengi*) in particular benefits from glycerine treatment.

Statice (*Limonium sinuatum*) is a trouble-free flower to dry by hanging, but if you want to have less brittle flowers, you can buy it fresh or cut it from the garden and stand the last 2 inches (5 cm) of the stems in glycerine solution for a few days. As soon as the papery flower heads feel soft they are ready to take out of the liquid. The shorter you cut the stems, the faster they soften. Hang upside down to dry.

PLANT MATERIAL PRESERVED IN GLYCERINE
SOME DOS & DON'TS

DO store it in an upright position whenever possible, in an area that is neither damp nor too warm.

DO store leaves, which have been preserved individually, between sheets of tissue paper.

DON'T store it in airtight containers. If it is stored in cardboard boxes, **DO** make air holes in them.

DON'T put silica gel in any container containing glycerine-preserved material.

DO store glycerine-preserved material by itself. If stored with dried-plant material, that dry material could absorb moisture from it.

DO wipe off any condensation that forms on the foliage, then wash it in warm water and dry it with a soft cloth. **DO** this and you will prevent mildew from forming on it.

Following are two lists of plants that can be successfully preserved in glycerine. The first gives the common name, then the Latin name, and any pertinent comments or tips. The second list gives the Latin name followed by the common name.

PLANTS THAT CAN BE PRESERVED IN GLYCERINE
COMMON NAME/*LATIN NAME*

Common Name	Latin Name	Comments
Barberry	*Berberis* spp	Wild and cultivated species
Bay	*Lauris nobilis*	Kitchen herb
Beech	*Fagus* spp	———
Bells-of-Ireland	*Moluccella laevis*	Total immersion is best
Blackberry; dewberry	*Rubus macropetalus*	Wild and cultivated plants
Box; boxwood	*Buxus* spp	Turns golden-yellow
Bracken	*Pteridium aquilinum*	A fern; rewarding to preserve
Broom, Scotch	*Cytisus scoparius*	———
Camellia, common	*Camellia japonica*	———
Clematis	*Clematis* spp	Garden and wild species
Cotoneaster	*Cotoneaster* spp	Hardy deciduous shrubs
Dogwood	*Cornus* spp	Illegal to pick in the wild
Dock	*Rumex* spp	Common weeds
Elaeagnus	*Elaeagnus* spp	Use evergreen species
Eucalyptus	*Eucalyptus* spp	Especially the "florist's" variety
Forsythia; golden-bells	*Forsythia* spp	———
Hawthorn	*Crataegus* spp	———
Heath	*Erica* spp	———
Heather	*Calluna* spp	———
Holly	*Ilex* spp	Most species & cultivars will preserve
Hop, common	*Humulus lupulus*	———
Hydrangea	*Hydrangea paniculata*	———
Ivy	*Hedera* spp & var.	Immerse strands to preserve
Laurel, Japanese	*Aucuba japonica*	Not to be confused with Bay
Laurel, mountain	*Kalmia latifolia*	Not to be confused with Bay
Laurel, Portugal	*Prunus lusitanica*	Not to be confused with Bay
Lime tree; linden	*Tilia* spp	Flowers and bracts preserve well
Lily-of-the-valley	*Convallaria majalis*	Immerse leaves only in solution
Magnolia	*Magnolia* spp	———
Maple	*Acer* spp	Many species, Japanese maple esp.
Montebretia	*Crocosmia crocosmiiflora*	Preserve the seed heads
Oak	*Quercus* spp	———
Old-man's-beard	*Clematis vitalba*	This is the wild clematis
Oregon grape	*Mahonia aquifolium*	———

☞

Common Name	Latin Name	Comments
Peony	*Paeonia officinalis*	Mature foliage and seed heads
Prunus	*Prunus* spp	Especially the dark-leaved varieties
Rhododendron; azalea	*Rhododendron* spp, var.,	Submerge individual leaves
Rosemary	*Rosmarinus officinalis*	Retains its perfume
Rowan	*Sorbus aucuparia*	Leaves and berries can be preserved
Rue, common	*Ruta graveolens*	One of the bitter herbs
Salal	*Gaultheria shallon*	Found in northwestern coastal forests
Viburnum; arrowwood	*Viburnum* spp	Ornamental shrubs
Willow	*Salix* spp	*S. tortuosa* has an interesting form

PLANTS THAT CAN BE PRESERVED IN GLYCERINE
LATIN NAME/COMMON NAME

Latin Name	Common Name	Latin Name	Common Name
Acer spp	Maple	*Hydrangea paniculata*	Hydrangea
Aucuba japonica	Laurel, Japanese	*Ilex* spp	Holly
Berberis spp	Barberry	*Kalmia latifolia*	Laurel, mountain
Buxus spp	Box; boxwood	*Laurus nobilis*	Bay
Calluna spp	Heather	*Magnolia* spp	Magnolia
Camellia japonica	Camellia, common	*Mahonia aquifolium*	Oregon grape
Clematis spp	Clematis	*Moluccella laevis*	Bells-of-Ireland
Clematis vitalba	Old-man's-beard	*Paeonia officinalis*	Peony
Convallaria majalis	Lily-of-the-valley	*Prunus lusitanica*	Laurel, Portugal
Cornus spp	Dogwood	*Prunus* spp	Prunus
Cotoneaster spp	Cotoneaster	*Pteridium aquilinum*	Bracken
Crataegus spp	Hawthorn	*Quercus* spp	Oak
Crocosmia crocosmiiflora	Montebretia	*Rhododendron* spp, var., & hybrids	Rhododendron; azalea
Cytisus scoparius	Broom, Scotch	*Rosmarinus officinalis*	Rosemary
Elaeagnus spp	Elaeagnus	*Rubus macropetalus*	Blackberry; dewberry
Erica spp	Heath	*Rumex* spp	Dock
Eucalyptus spp	Eucalyptus	*Ruta graveolens*	Rue, common
Fagus spp	Beech	*Salix* spp	Willow
Forsythia spp	Forsythia; golden-bells	*Sorbus aucuparia*	Rowan
Gaultheria shallon	Salal	*Tilia* spp	Lime tree; linden
Hedera spp & var.	Ivy	*Viburnum* spp	Viburnum; arrowwood
Humulus lupulus	Hop, common		

Pressing Plant Material

METHODS 16–18

A S ALWAYS, be sure that any plant material you want to press is quite dry when it is gathered. Pick the material in the late morning or early afternoon after it has had a few hours of sunshine, but preferably after two or three consecutive sunny days. Do not leave the material lying around to wilt—press it immediately.

You will need a lot of old newspapers, tissues and/or blotting paper, sand, bricks, or other heavy weights. You will also need thick catalogs, telephone directories, or old heavy books (visit a thrift store or secondhand bookshop for out-of-date encyclopedias and other such tomes). Or you can make a flower press such as the one shown on page 121, which will give you the best results because the pressure exerted by it is absolutely even, holding the absorbent paper firmly against the material being pressed. Unlike books, a press full of drying plant material can be moved without fear of upset.

HOW TO PRESS FLOWERS IN A BOOK
METHOD 16

Open the book a few pages from one end and lay a tissue of folded piece of blotting paper on the page. Gently crush the center of the flower to be pressed between your thumb and first finger. If the flower has a hard calyx you can either cut it out or press it between sheets of wax paper with a cold iron. Lay the flowers on the tissue or blotting paper so they do not touch. Petals that overlap each other naturally can be left that way, but be careful to lay them flat and don't allow them to double under. Cover with another tissue or close them between a folded sheet of blotting paper. Turn over about ten pages and repeat this procedure until the book is full. Pile heavy weights on top: bricks, cans of sand, or several heavy books are all suitable. Leave for a day or two, then open the book carefully. If the tissues or blotting paper look damp, lift the flowers with stamp tweezers and place them on fresh tissues or blotting paper in the book. Put the flowers back to continue pressing. In about two weeks they should be dry. If you do not want to use them immediately they can be stored in the book.

Remember that nothing you press will be three-dimensional, so try to vary the shapes of the material, press a few buds, and some flowers in profile.

HOW TO PRESS LEAVES
METHOD 17

Pressing is undoubtedly the best way to preserve the color of fall leaves. Usually the color of individual leaves can be fixed by following the procedure outlined above for pressing flowers. Some leaves retain their color better, however, if they are placed on a newspaper, covered with a paper towel, and pressed with a fairly hot iron. Press them further between newspapers with a weight on top and they should be dry in two weeks. They can be stored between the pages of the newspaper if they are not needed immediately.

If you want to dry **whole branches of leaves**, choose those with leaves that lie flat naturally. Spread them out on newspapers; try to avoid overlapping the leaves. Put the whole packet under a carpet in an area of heavy traffic or under a firm mattress. You can store them right there until they're needed.

The **time to gather leaves and branches** depends on the color you want the dried leaves to be. Picked green, they will retain that color, and so on through yellow to the vibrant colors of fall.

Bracken is particularly rewarding to press. Use the small lateral shoots because they are easier to handle. Be sure to pick perfectly flat undamaged specimens, put them between layers of newspaper, then place a weight on top of them. You can pick them young and green or wait until they have turned gold or even brown—they will all retain their color well. In about two weeks the green leaves will be dry; the yellow ones will be ready more quickly; and the brown ones will need no drying, only pressing.

IF YOU ARE IN A HURRY
METHOD 18

If your need for pressed leaves or flowers is immediate, prepare them in the same way you would for long-term pressing. After they have been under weights for a few hours, lay them in a pan with 1 inch (2.5 cm) of silica gel directly under and on top of them, put weights on top, and leave overnight. If you can't wait until the next day, pop the container with silica gel (the weights won't be necessary) in the microwave oven for 1 minute on high. Let it stand to cool for half an hour, then pour off the silica gel.

HOW TO MAKE A PRESS FOR FLOWERS AND LEAVES

To make a press for flowers and leaves you will need some plywood, four bolts with wing nuts and washers, some newspapers, and sheets of blotting paper (Figure 8).

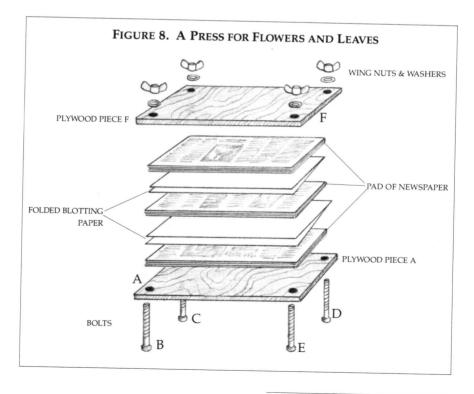

FIGURE 8. A PRESS FOR FLOWERS AND LEAVES

WING NUTS & WASHERS

PLYWOOD PIECE F — F

PAD OF NEWSPAPER

FOLDED BLOTTING PAPER

PLYWOOD PIECE A

A

BOLTS — B C D E

A convenient small-size press would measure about 10 by 14 inches (25 by 35 cm), which is the size the two pieces of plywood should be. Bore a hole in each corner, about 1/2 inch (2.5 cm) from the edges, large enough to take the bolts. The length of the bolts depends on the thickness you want your press to be. The longer they are, the more sheets of blotting paper (and flowers) you will be able to get between the two sheets of plywood. Assembly instructions are as follows.

1) Place the four bolts—B, C, D, E—through the holes in plywood-piece A.
2) Put a few sheets of newspaper on A (cut a little smaller than the sheets of plywood).
3) Put a piece of blotting paper, folded in half, on the newspaper.
4) Place the material to be pressed between the folded blotting paper. Keep materials of similar thickness in the same layer (Figure 9).

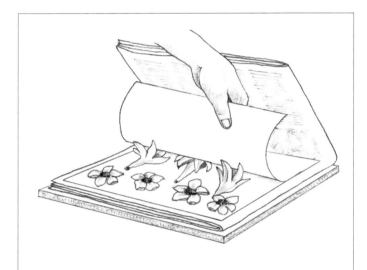

▲ **FIGURE 9.** Place the material to be pressed between folded blotting paper. Roll the blotting paper *gently* over the flowers so that the flowers do not become dislodged or overlap.

5) Cover with a few more newspapers.
6) Continue making a "sandwich" of plant material, blotting paper, and newspapers.

7) Top the whole thing with the lid, plywood-piece F.
8) Screw the wing nuts down securely. Check the tightness of the wing nuts daily and keep them tight.
9) Keep the press in a warm dry room.
10) You can check the material after a few days, but unless the blotting paper is damp, do not disturb it. If it *is* damp it should be changed *with the greatest care.*
11) The plant material will probably be dry in about two to three weeks, depending on the moisture content of the plant material.
12) Always keep the pressed material out of the sun and away from fluorescent lights.

ð   ð   ð

Pressing flowers and leaves is a subject that could be discussed at much greater length. This short section is just to get you started and give you some ideas. Calendars, book markers, notes and greeting cards, place mats, menu cards, and trays can all be made attractive with pressed flowers and leaves. You can also "paint" pictures using pressed plant material; see the section with pressed flowers and leaves projects.

ð   ð   ð

The two lists that follow give the Latin names and common names and any tips or comments for some *flowers* that press well. There are, of course, many more than those listed below. Experiment with what you have available in your garden or can obtain from a florist. In theory, most flowers can be pressed, but the criterion for choosing is based on how well the colors are retained when the procedure is complete.

FLOWERS THAT PRESS WELL
COMMON NAME/*LATIN NAME*

Common Name	Latin Name	Comments
Auricula	*Primula auricula*	Petals have many different colors
Basket-of-gold	*Aurinia saxatilis*	Retains yellow color well
Bear's-breech	*Acanthus* spp	Retains purple color well
Blackberry; dewberry	*Rubus macropetalus*	Flowers are a delicate mauve-white
Bleeding-heart	*Dicentra spectabilis*	Interesting shapes
Bracken	*Pteridium aquilinum*	Very useful foliage
Buttercup, common	*Ranunculus acris*	Beautiful texture and gold color
California poppy	*Eschscholzia californica*	Press individual petals
Calliopsis	*Coreopsis tinctoria*	Retains yellow color well
Christmas rose	*Helleborus niger*	Retains its interesting texture when pressed
Chrysanthemum	*Chrysanthemum* spp	Press any petals of unusual shape
Clematis	*Clematis* spp & var.	Press wild and garden varieties
Columbine	*Aquilegia* spp	Press unusual shapes
Coneflower	*Rudbeckia* spp	Press petals separately
Crocus, autumn	*Colchicum autumnale*	Press petals separately
Dahlia	*Dahlia* spp & var.	Press petals with interesting shapes
Delphinium	*Delphinium* spp & var.	Petals have interesting shapes
Dusty Miller	*Senecio cineraria*	Florists often sell this plant in pots
Freesia	*Freesia* x *hybrida*	Press flat or open
Gentian	*Gentiana acaulis*	Beautiful blue color
Geranium	*Pelargonium zonale*	Retains red shades well
Golden marguerite	*Anthemis tinctoria*	Press individual petals
Goldenrod	*Solidago* spp	Press small pieces
Heath	*Erica* spp	Tiny flowers press well
Heather; Scotch heather	*Calluna vulgaris*	Tiny flowers press well
Hydrangea	*Hydrangea paniculata*	Keeps color well
Larkspur	*Consolida regalis*	Petals have interesting shapes
Lobelia	*Lobelia* spp & var.	Use blue varieties
Mallowwort	*Malope* spp	Deep pink petals; press individually
Marigold, pot	*Calendula officinalis*	Pot and medicinal herb
Montebretia	*Crocosmia crocosmiiflora*	Retains orange color well
Pansy; violet	*Viola* spp & var.	Small dark ones retain color well

Common Name	Latin Name	Comments
Primrose, English	*Primula vulgaris*	Dainty pale yellow flowers
Purple coneflower	*Echinacea purpurea*	Press individual petals
Sage, blue	*Salvia azurea*	A half-hardy blue salvia
Tulips	*Tulipa* spp	Retains texture and lasts a long time
Wallflower	*Cheiranthus cheiri*	Yellow and bronze flowers press well
Windflower	*Anemone* spp	Press petals separately
Yellow oxeye	*Telekia speciosa*	Press yellow petals separately

PLANTS THAT PRESS WELL
LATIN NAME/COMMON NAME

Latin Name	Common Name	Latin Name	Common Name
Acanthus spp	Bear's-breech	*Eschscholzia californica*	California poppy
Anemone spp	Windflower	*Freesia* x *hybrida*	Freesia
Anthemis tinctoria	Golden margeurite	*Gentiana acaulis*	Gentian
Aquilegia spp	Columbine	*Helleborus niger*	Christmas rose
Aurinia saxatilis	Basket-of-gold	*Hydrangea paniculata*	Hydrangea
Calendula officinalis	Marigold, pot	*Lobelia* spp & var.	Lobelia
Calluna vulgaris	Heather; Scotch heather	*Malope* spp	Mallowwort
Cheiranthus cheiri	Wallflower	*Pelargonium zonale*	Geranium
Chrysanthemum spp	Chrysanthemum	*Primula auricula*	Auricula
Clematis spp & var.	Clematis	*Primula vulgaris*	Primrose, English
Consolida regalis	Larkspur	*Pteridium aquilinum*	Bracken
Coreopsis tinctoria	Calliopsis	*Ranunculus acris*	Buttercup, common
Colchicum autumnale	Crocus, autumn	*Rubus macropetalus*	Blackberry; dewberry
Crocosmia crocosmiiflora	Montebretia	*Rudbeckia* spp	Coneflower
Dahlia spp & var.	Dahlia	*Salvia azurea*	Sage, blue
Delphinium spp & var.	Delphinium	*Senecio cineraria*	Dusty Miller
Dicentra spectabilis	Bleeding-heart	*Solidago* spp	Goldenrod
Echinacea purpurea	Purple coneflower	*Telekia speciosa*	Yellow oxeye
Erica spp	Heath	*Tulipa* spp	Tulip
		Viola spp & var.	Pansy; violet

SEED HEADS & SEEDPODS

NATURE'S BONUS

THERE WILL BE SEED HEADS and seedpods free for the collecting in your garden, in the fields, on the roadside, and wherever plants grow. Keep your eyes open, especially in the late summer and early fall, and you will find an unlimited supply of seed heads and pods for your collection of dried plant materials. Try picking them at different stages of maturity, whenever the color and shapes are interesting.

As any gardener knows, allowing perennial plants and bulbs to go to seed can weaken their future growth. They should all be dead-headed (the removal, by pinching or cutting, of dead or faded flowers) long before seedpods even start to form. But collectors of dried plant material can be forgiven for allowing one or two perennial flowers per plant to produce seed heads, or even allow the flower of a bulb to produce its unusual seedpods.

Annual flowers are different because their lives end when they go to seed. Therefore, the seed heads or seedpods of annual plants can be picked at whatever stage of maturity you wish. Either green immature pods, yellow half-ripe pods, or fully ripe ones, it doesn't matter as far as the future health and vigor of the plant are concerned.

You can, of course, grow a garden especially for the seedpods that will be reaped. It would not be an attractive garden because it would look as though it had been neglected. So put such a garden in a corner or an out-of-the-way place where it won't offend the eye or your gardening sensibilities.

Most seedheads and pods can be stored and preserved easily as soon as you collect them. Just hang them (Method 1) or stand them upright in cans or Oasis (Methods 2 or 4). Those you have picked green may be hung (Method 1) or treated with glycerine (Method 15).

Don't forget that many plants produce a variety of cones, nuts, or berries, which can also be attractive in dried arrangements. In warm dry weather, dry cones outside, but do not put them in the sun. Indoors, dry them near a furnace (Method 5) or in a cupboard around a hot water tank (Method 8). Do not crowd them because they often expand as they dry.

IF YOU COLLECT MATERIAL FROM WILD PLANTS

- Check local conservation laws first for plants on the endangered species list, so you won't mistakenly pick them.
- Always leave more pods on the plant than you take.
- Give the seed heads a good shake to distribute some of the seeds around the plants.
- *Cut* the stem you want, *don't pull it off*. Pulling could damage the plant roots. Be especially careful with perennial plants.

Two lists of plants follow. The first list gives the common names of plants with interesting seed heads or seedpods, in alphabetical order, followed by the Latin names, and identifications of the plant type. The second gives the Latin names in alphabetical order followed by the common names. There are both wild and garden plants in each list. They are, of course, not the only plants that have interesting seed heads or pods, but these lists will help get you started as you go about collecting such materials.

Many alpine and rock plants, both wild and garden varieties, have interesting seed heads, which are delightful when dried and used in miniature arrangements. An excellent book on this subject is *Rock Garden and Alpine Plants* by David Joyce and published by Arco.

PLANTS WITH INTERESTING SEED HEADS

1. Poppy seed heads (*Papaver* spp)
2. Dill (*Anethum graveolens*)
3. "Fruit" of *Iris* species
4. Columbine (*Aquilegia* spp)
5. Sedge (*Carex* spp)
6. Common rue (*Ruta graveolens*)
7. Old-man's-beard (*Clematis vitalba*)

PLANTS WITH INTERESTING SEED HEADS

1. Fennel (*Foeniculum vulgare*)
2. Eryngo (*Eryngium* spp)
3. Honesty (*Lunaria annua*)

4. Common wheat (*Triticum aestivum*)
5. Hare's-tail grass (*Lagurus ovatus*)
6. Onion (*Allium cepa*)

PLANTS THAT HAVE INTERESTING SEED HEADS OR SEEDPODS
COMMON NAME/*LATIN NAME*

Common Name	Latin Name	Plant Type
Aconite, winter	*Eranthis hyemalis*	Hardy bulbs
African lily	*Agapanthus africanus*	Rhizomatous; propagated by division
Alyssum, sweet	*Lobularia maritima*	Annual; grown from seed
Anemone; windflower	*Anemone coronaria*	Hardy bulb
Angelica	*Angelica archangelica*	Biennial herb; propagate by seed
Bear's-breech	*Acanthus* spp	Hardy perennial
Bluebell, English	*Endymion non-scriptus*	Wild, hardy bulb
Blue false indigo	*Baptisia australis*	Hardy perennial
Blue lace flower	*Trachymene coerulea*	Annual; grown from seed
Bouncing bet	*Saponaria officinalis*	Hardy perennial
Burning bush; gas plant	*Dictamnus albus*	Hardy perennial
Canterbury-bells	*Campanula medium*	Hardy perennial
Cattail, common	*Typha latifolia*	Wild; found in ditches
Chervil	*Anthriscus cerefolium*	Annual herb
Chinese-lantern plant	*Physalis alkekengi*	Hardy perennial
Chive	*Allium schoenoprasum*	Hardy perennial herb
Clarkia	*Clarkia* spp	Annuals; grown from seed
Clematis	*Clematis* spp	Hardy perennials; climbers
Columbine	*Aquilegia* spp	Hardy perennials
Cress, American; cress, early winter	*Barbarea verna*	Edible hardy perennial
Cress, field penny	*Thlaspi arvense*	Wild, common, annual weed
Crown-imperial	*Fritillaria imperialis*	Hardy bulb
Cupid's-dart	*Catanache caerulea*	Hardy perennial
Delphinium	*Delphinium* spp & var.	Hardy perennials
Dill	*Anethum graveolens*	Annual herb
Dock; sorrel	*Rumex* spp	Hardy perennials; wild
Fennel	*Foeniculum vulgare*	Hardy perennial herb
Foxglove(s)	*Digitalis* spp	Hardy biennial
Gas plant; burning bush	*Dictamnus albus*	See Burning bush
Gladiolus	*Gladiolus* spp & var.	Half-hardy biennial bulbs
Globe thistle, small	*Echinops ritro*	Hardy perennial

Common Name	Latin Name	Plant Type
Goat's-beard; Jack-go-to-bed-at-noon	*Tragopogon pratensis*	Biennial; wild
Grape hyacinth	*Muscari* spp & var.	Hardy bulbs
Hellebore	*Helleborus* spp	Hardy perennials
Hollyhock	*Alcea rosea*	Hardy perennial
Honesty	*Lunaria annua*	Hardy biennial
Iris	*Iris* spp	Hardy perennial rhizome; also propagated by seed
Iris, scarlet-seeded; iris, stinking	*Iris foetidissima*	Very interesting pods
Jerusalem sage	*Phlomis fruticosa*	Hardy shrub
Joe-Pye-weed	*Eupatorium purpureum*	Hardy perennial weed
Knapweed	*Centaurea* spp	Perennial and annual weeds
Knotweed	*Polygonum* spp	Hardy annual weeds
Larkspur	*Consolida regalis*	Hardy annual
Leek, garden	*Allium ampeloprasum* (Porrum Group)	Biennial vegetable
Love-in-a-mist; wild fennel	*Nigella damascena*	Hardy annual
Lily	*Lilium* spp	Hardy and half-hardy bulbs
Lupine	*Lupinus* spp & var.	Hardy perennials and annuals
Mallow	*Malva* spp	Hardy perennials
Milkweed	*Asclepias* spp	Hardy and half-hardy perennials
Okra	*Abelmoschus esculentus*	Half-hardy perennial
Onion	*Allium cepa*	Hardy perennial; grown as an annual
Onion, edible	*Allium* spp	Onions, leeks, chives, etc.
Onion, ornamental	*Allium* spp	Hardy perennials
Onion, wild	*Allium* spp	Hardy perennials
Orach	*Atriplex hortensis*	Hardy annual
Peony, common garden	*Paeonia lactiflora* var.	Hardy perennial
Pincushions	*Scabiosa atropurpurea* var.	Hardy annual
Poppy	*Papaver* spp & var.	Hardy annuals, biennials, and perennials
Queen-Anne's-lace	*Daucus carota*	Hardy biennial
Queen-of-the-meadow	*Filipendula ulmaria*	Hardy perennial
Red-hot-poker	*Kniphofia uvaria*	Hardy perennial

Common Name	Latin Name	Plant Type
Rhododendron	*Rhododendron* spp & var.	Hardy shrubs
Rose-of-Sharon	*Hibiscus syriacus*	Hardy shrub
Rose-of-Sharon	*Hypericum calycinum*	Hardy perennial shrub
Rue, common	*Ruta graveolens*	Hardy perennial shrub
Rush	*Juncus* spp	Hardy perennials
Sage, mealy-cup	*Salvia farinacea*	Half-hardy annual
Sedge	*Carex* spp	Hardy perennials
Shepherd's-purse	*Capsella bursa-pastoris*	Hardy annual, common weed
Squill	*Scilla* spp	Hardy bulbs
Snapdragon, common	*Antirrhinum majus*	Half-hardy annual
Sorrel; dock	*Rumex* spp	Hardy perennials; wild, edible
St.-John's-wort	*Hypericum* spp	Hardy perennial
Sweet Cicely; myrrh	*Myrrhis odorata*	Hardy perennial herb
Tansy, common	*Tanacetum vulgare*	Hardy perennial herb
Teasel	*Dipsacus sativus*	Hardy biennial
Thistle	*Cirsium* spp	Mostly biennials
Tulip	*Tulipa* spp & var.	Hardy bulbs
Witch hazel	*Hamamelis* spp	Hardy trees
Yucca	*Yucca* spp	Hardy and half-hardy perennials

PLANTS THAT HAVE INTERESTING SEED HEADS OR SEEDPODS
LATIN NAME/COMMON NAME

Latin Name	Common Name	Latin Name	Common Name
Abelmoschus esculentus	Okra	*Allium* spp	Onion (edible)
Acanthus montanus	Bear's-breech	*Allium* spp	Onion (ornamental)
Agapanthus africanus	African lily	*Allium* spp	Onion (wild)
Alcea rosea	Hollyhock	*Anemone coronaria*	Anemone; wind-flower
Allium ampeloprasum (Porrum Group)	Leek, garden	*Anethum graveolens*	Dill
Allium cepa	Onion	*Angelica archangelica*	Angelica
Allium schoenoprasum	Chive	*Anthriscus cerefolium*	Chervil

Latin Name	Common Name	Latin Name	Common Name
Antirrhinum majus	Snapdragon, common	*Iris* spp	Iris
Aquilegia spp	Columbine	*Iris foetidissima*	Iris, scarlet-seeded; stinking iris
Asclepias spp	Milkweed	*Juncus* spp	Rush
Atriplex hortensis	Orach	*Kniphofia uvaria*	Red-hot-poker
Baptisia australis	Blue false indigo	*Lilium* spp	Lily
Barbarea verna	Cress, American; early winter cress	*Lobularia maritima*	Alyssum, sweet
		Lunaria annua	Honesty
Campanula medium	Canterbury-bells	*Lupinus* spp & var.	Lupine
Capsella bursa-pastoris	Shepherd's-purse	*Malva* spp	Mallow
Carex spp	Sedge	*Muscari* spp & var.	Grape hyacinth
Catanache caerulea	Cupid's-dart	*Myrrhis odorata*	Sweet Cicely; myrrh
Centaurea spp	Knapweed		
Cirsium spp	Thistle	*Nigella damascena*	Love-in-a-mist; wild fennel
Clarkia spp	Clarkia		
Clematis spp	Clematis	*Paeonia lactiflora* var.	Peony, common garden
Consolida regalis	Larkspur		
Daucus carota	Queen-Anne's-lace	*Papaver* spp & var.	Poppy
Delphinium spp & var.	Delphinium	*Phlomis fruticosa*	Jerusalem sage
Dictamnus albus	Burning bush; gas plant	*Physalis alkekengi*	Chinese-lantern plant
		Polygonum spp	Knotweed
Digitalis spp	Foxglove(s)	*Rhododendron* spp & var.	Rhododendron
Dipsacus sativus	Teasel	*Rumex* spp	Sorrel; dock
Echinops ritro	Globe thistle, small	*Ruta graveolens*	Rue, common
Endymion non-scriptus	Bluebell, English	*Salvia farinacea*	Mealy-cup sage
Eranthis hyemalis	Aconite, winter	*Saponaria officinalis*	Bouncing bet
Eupatorium purpureum	Joe-Pye-weed	*Scabiosa atropurpurea* var.	Pincushions
Filipendula ulmaria	Queen-of-the-meadow	*Scilla* spp	Squill
Foeniculum vulgare	Fennel	*Tanacetum vulgare*	Tansy, common
Fritillaria imperialis	Crown-imperial	*Thlaspi arvense*	Cress, field penny
Gladiolus spp & var.	Gladiolus	*Trachymene coerulea*	Blue lace flower
Hamamelis spp	Witch hazel	*Tragopogon pratensis*	Goat's-beard; Jack-go-to-bed-at-noon
Helleborus spp	Hellebore		
Hibiscus syriacus	Rose-of-Sharon	*Tulipa* spp & var.	Tulip
Hypericum calycinum	Rose-of-Sharon	*Typha latifolia*	Cattail, common
Hypericum spp	St.-John's-wort	*Yucca* spp	Yucca

PART III

THE PERPETUAL ENJOYMENT OF EVERLASTINGS

MECHANICS, DISPLAY, CARE, STORAGE, PROJECTS

Drawings by Judy Eliason

TOOLS, SUPPLIES,
& OTHER NECESSARY THINGS

MANY OF THE ITEMS needed to make best use of everlasting plants are listed on the pages that follow and can be found in any household. Others will only be found where there is an enthusiastic flower arranger. A few you will have to make a special effort to find, but you may be able to beg or borrow them from friends!

Try to reserve a corner in your house where you can leave all your tools and materials undisturbed. The ideal place would be close to the storage area for your dried plant material. Such a place would have a cupboard or two, a table with a drawer, and/or a countertop. Don't forget a comfortable stool or chair. In damp climates a dehumidifier is invaluable.

TOOLS

BRUSHES. Either a camel-hair paintbrush or a photographer's lens brush for removing desiccants from delicate flower petals.

ELECTRIC FRYING PAN. To melt Hot Glue. The frying pan only needs to get warm, so one that does not get hot enough to cook with will be sufficient. Look around in thrift shops or garage sales if you haven't got an old one that is no longer any use in the kitchen. Obviously whatever pan you use to melt glue can never again be used to prepare food.

HAMMER. A heavy one for crushing tough stem ends.

KNIVES. *A long-bladed kitchen knife* for cutting floral foam and Styrofoam; a *utility knife* with renewable blades will be useful; and a *putty knife*, which is invaluable for removing floral clay from containers.

NEEDLES. *Knitting needles* of various small gauges for making holes in foam. When smaller holes are needed use *coarse sewing needles*.

PUTTY KNIFE. See Knives

SCISSORS. Several pairs, both small and large, with blunt and pointed tips.

SECATEURS (PRUNING SHEARS). Gardener's secateurs will cut material too tough for ordinary shears or scissors, but do *not* use them to cut wire.

SHEARS, FLORIST. The loop-handled type are comfortable to use.

SKEWERS. When sewing or knitting needles are not suitable for making holes in foam, fine poultry skewers will also do the job.

SPOON. A slotted kitchen spoon will be useful for removing dried material from silica gel.

STAPLE GUN. Used by carpenters and home handymen, it effectively secures plant material to many different kinds of surfaces.

TWEEZERS. Those used by stamp collectors (with rounded heads and milled grips) will not damage the material being picked up.

WIRE CUTTERS. *Always* use this small hand-held tool to cut wire—*never* use ordinary scissors—though some *floral* scissors have a special notch, which will be obvious, for cutting wire.

SUPPLIES

BOUQUET HOLDERS. These little plastic holders have foam centers into which you can push the stems of dried flowers to make a dainty bouquet.

CEMENTS. *Contact cement* for sticking pressed flowers securely to their backgrounds (only the tiniest dot of adhesive should be put on the underside of leaves or flowers). *Transparent china cement* will secure wire to natural plant stems.

CLAY, FLORIST'S. Used to secure pinholders to the bottom of containers.

FOAM, FLORAL. Sometimes you will use regular (or wet) Oasis, but more often Oasis Sec (Sahara) and Ultra Foam.

GLUE GUN. This can be used to spot stick heavy plant material.

GLUES. *Hot Glue* will stick dried-plant material to almost any surface or stick any type of foam to most containers. Clear *photo glue* should be used for delicate jobs, such as reattaching damaged petals when they have come off at the base of the flower; it is available at photographic or frame shops (where it is used to mount photos) or at a photographer's supply store. Generic *white glue* can be used for many of the sticking jobs you will have.

NETTING, WIRE. A plastic-coated wire netting is more pliable and durable than chicken wire, but more expensive. Either type is useful to have on hand.

PICKS. Toothpicks and floral picks are sometimes used to reinforce or replace stems.

PINHOLDERS (also called frog pins or kenzan). You will need both regular and needlepoint pinholders; either plastic or leadbased or both. Some pinholders have an outer cage and these are useful if your plant material needs extra support.

PLASTER OF PARIS. A lump of it in an otherwise top-heavy container will help stabilize the container, and hopefully, prevent accidents.

PLASTIC ADHESIVES, CLEAR. Mac Tac is one brand that comes in an 18-inch (45-cm) width and is suitable for sealing pressed flower projects (see pages 181 and 182, 191 and 192). Another type, from Germany, is Teneca; available in 8-inch (20-cm), 12-inch (30-cm), and 16-inch (40-cm) widths.

SPRAYS, PRESERVATIVE. Dri-Seal is made specifically for dried-plant material. Krylon is a clear plastic spray (my can says "contains no fluorocarbons") that has numerous applications, including the preservation of everlasting plants. In addition, any clear acrylic spray purchased at a craft store or, failing all of these, a "regular hold" hair spray will do.

STYROFOAM. This very firm foam comes in many shapes and sizes. It is useful for freestanding and hanging plant arrangements.

TAPES. Regular *medical adhesive tapes* of various widths are employed when a very firm hold is needed. *Cloth-coated tape* is valuable to have when a very firm hold is needed and it is going to show. It comes in several suitable colors. *Floral tape* to cover wires, to reinforce brittle stems, and to tape two or more stems together. Available in several colors, of which brown and green are essential. It is flexible and stretchy. The half-inch width is the most useful, but other widths are available. *Freezer* or *masking tape* can be used for securing foam to containers and making pictures airtight. *Scotch tape*—what would we do without it? And let me recommend Magic Plus, which is reusable.

WAX, CANNING. Parowax (or similar canning waxes) can be used to seal the stem ends of plant material preserved with glycerine.

WIRE. Gauges 18, 20, 22, and 24 will fulfill your minimum requirements. Buy small packets (weighing about 2 ounces each) of the longest length available. Cut off the length of wire you need as you need it; this is more economical than buying different lengths of each thickness. A roll of gauge 34 will be useful for binding stems together.

THINGS TO COLLECT

BOXES WITH LIDS. Cardboard shoe boxes, florist's boxes, dress boxes, plastic freezer boxes, or any good box with a lid will be invaluable for drying and storage.

CONES (from trees). All shapes and sizes can be used.

CYLINDERS, CARDBOARD. Mailing cylinders can be used for drying tall straight stems, such as upright rosemary, in a desiccant. Save the cylinders from paper towels and toilet paper as well—they can support desiccant-dried material in storage.

DRIFTWOOD. Interesting shapes can be used in arrangements, and sometimes you may even find pieces that can be used as a container.

FRAMES FROM OLD LAMP SHADES. Plants with pliable stems, such as the brooms, can be tied to these frames while they are drying. This will give them an attractive curve.

FRAMES, PICTURE. Search in thrift shops, secondhand or antique shops for old photo and picture frames (you may have to buy the picture as well!). All the parts are useful: the backs and glass as well as the frame.

GLASS. Crushed glass from broken automobile *windows*, not windshield glass. Available at a car wrecker's place of business, it should be free.

MARBLES. Clear and colored are useful.

MOSSES. Many different kinds of moss can be dried and used to cover the base of an arrangement or to hide the mechanics. Stick it to the base with contact cement or Hot Glue; if you are using a foam base, pin it in place with U-shaped wires. Sphagnum moss is one of the most useful and easily obtained (often found on rocks in the woods). Spread it to dry in a cool airy place and store it, loosely packed, in open boxes.

PEBBLES AND STONES. Collect all shapes and sizes to use in the bottom of containers for weight and stability. They can also be used to create the illusion of a rugged environment.

PLASTIC FREEZER BOXES WITH LIDS. To store dried-plant material.

SAND AND SMALL GRAVEL. These can both be used to weight containers and to help hold stems in place.

TINS. Collect all shapes and sizes that have fitted airtight lids. Coffee tins are excellent and so are English biscuit tins (if you can find them). Thrift shops are a good source for these.

CONTAINERS AND BASES

When choosing containers to hold arrangements of dried-plant material, basically the same principles apply as when you are using fresh flowers, but your scope is much wider. It is important for the containers to harmonize with the dried plant material and not overpower it.

Visit thrift shops, garage sales, and craft sales, as well as second-hand and antique stores. Shop for interesting shapes in a variety of materials and sizes, remembering that the heavier the base of the container the easier it will be to use. With a little ingenuity you can even disguise faults and change colors. Remember, too, that because the containers do not have to hold water, cracked and damaged ones will often do. Here are a few ideas to get you started.

BASKETS or **WICKER WARE.** Be sure that they're clean or they will detract from the freshness of the dried flowers.

BOARDS, CHEESE or **BREAD BOARDS.** Covered with a coarse material, they make a good base for hanging plaques.

CANDLESTICKS, CANDELABRA, and **WINE BOTTLES** can all be used if they are fitted with candle cups (Figure 10).

CONTAINERS of every description will be useful. Those made of pottery with glazed or unglazed interiors, iron stone, pewter, brass, and copper. Sugar bowls, rice bowls, onion soup bowls, soup tureens, compote dishes, earthenware pitchers and jugs, and brandy snifters, to name just a few.

For *miniature arrangements* use similarly-sized containers: egg cups, Chinese soup spoons, wine glasses, and shells (those of scallops and oysters especially). For the tiniest flowers use walnut shells and acorn cups. Stick a small piece of foam into

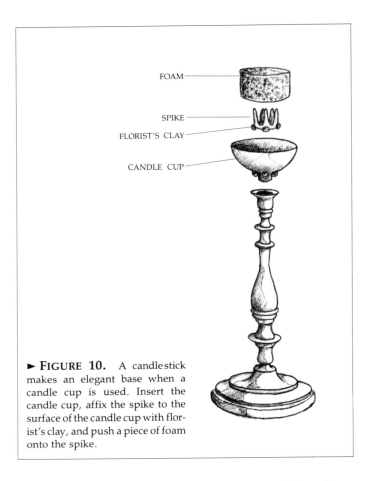

FOAM

SPIKE

FLORIST'S CLAY

CANDLE CUP

► **FIGURE 10.** A candlestick makes an elegant base when a candle cup is used. Insert the candle cup, affix the spike to the surface of the candle cup with florist's clay, and push a piece of foam onto the spike.

these tiny containers so that the stems can be held in place.

Plastic jugs and *bottles* can be used as containers. Just cut to whatever shape you need and paint them with a matte-finish paint. Their surface can be also be disguised with a coat of rough plaster, but work fast because it dries quickly. Be sure to weight them down—they can be unstable.

Shallow containers are good for making Oriental arrangements. At a craft shop, you can buy shallow plastic dishes made specifically to hold a block of foam securely; a spike can be attached to a pie plate or a cake pan with floral clay or glue and a block of foam speared onto it; or you can attach a pin-holder to a low-sided bowl with floral clay.

FIGURINES can be made the center of an arrangement. Cracks and chips can be hidden with a leaf or flower.

SMALL TRAYS can be used as bases and so can *thin flat slabs of stone,* though these are often hard to find.

A TREE TRUNK SLICE (whatever width you like or can get) makes a wonderful base. Apply felt to the bottom to protect the surface on which it will be placed and to prevent slipping. Secure the anchoring material (foam, pinholder) or container in which the plant material will be arranged.

How to Support
Dried-Plant Material

O NCE, FLOWER ARRANGERS had only sand and pebbles to help them stabilize their plant material in containers. Later, chicken wire was used. More recently pinholders were invented, and now we have many different kinds of foams as well. These, and other mechanics, are described on the pages that follow.

FLORAL FOAM

With the coming of floral foams, the task of the dried-flower arranger has been greatly simplified. The regular (or wet) oasis used for flower arrangements that need water is suitable only for the lightest dried flowers—those which have thin stems—either natural or wired ones. Floral foam sold under the trade name Oasis Sec or Sahara is suitable for anchoring and supporting almost all dried-plant material, including heavier items; the only exceptions are very heavy and thick-stemmed materials. Ultra Foam is thicker and harder than either Oasis Sec or Sahara and stands up better when stems have to be frequently pulled in and out of it.

Regular Oasis is usually green, Oasis Sec is green, Ultra Foam is paler green, and Sahara is brown.

All foam comes in rectangular blocks that measure 3-by-4-by-10 inches (7.5-by-10-by-25 cm). Ultra Foam also comes in sheets that are either 1 or 2 inches (2.5 to 5 cm) thick and 18 or 24 inches (45 to 60 cm) square. All are easy to cut with a large, sharp kitchen knife to any shape you need.

HOW TO USE FLORAL FOAM

Always handle floral foam gently, especially the regular (wet) Oasis. Undue pressure as you push it onto the mouth of a container could cause damage. Sometimes, depending on the shape of the container, it is better to push the container onto the foam, rather than trying to push the foam into the mouth of the container.

Whichever foam you choose, it must be made secure in the container. Cut it with a knife to fit into the mouth of the container or vase. Leave a little bit of it showing above the top so that the stems can be inserted at any angle you desire—one of the joys of using floral foam (Figure 11). Remember that only a short length of stem needs to be pushed into the foam for it to be held securely. Extra weight should be added before the foam is fitted in place, except in wide-mouthed bowls and flat dishes. These types of containers need two strips of tape over the foam to secure it in place (Figure 12). To arrange heavy

▲ **FIGURE 11.** Cut floral foam so that it fits snugly in the mouth of the container and be sure to leave a portion exposed to allow you maximum flexibility when arranging dried flowers and plants.

▲ **FIGURE 12.** When using wide or shallow containers, the floral foam will need to be secured with two strips of tape before you begin an arrangement. You can then complete the arrangement so that the tape is concealed.

material it is sometimes necessary to use wire netting over the foam for extra support, as described on page 148.

All foams can be secured to bases or containers with Hot Glue.

STYROFOAM

A very firm coarse foam, Styrofoam is suitable for securing heavy material that has natural stems or artificial wire stems. Use it to make freestanding and hanging plant arrangements. To insert woody stems, it will be necessary to make a hole in the Styrofoam with a thick sewing needle or a fine knitting needle before pushing in the plant stem. Be careful not to make the hole too big or too deep.

It is *not* suitable for fragile-stemmed material because their stems will not withstand the pressure of being placed into Styrofoam.

Styrofoam can be bought in blocks or previously cut into many shapes and sizes.

WEIGHTS AND FILLERS

Pebbles and stones, sand and grit (as is used in fishbowls), marbles, lead weights, and crushed automobile window glass can all be used to add weight to a container and so give stability to arrangements of dried plant material that would otherwise be top heavy. Heavy pin-holders also add some weight, and there are containers with hollow bases that can be filled with plaster. None of these is necessary if you are using a container that already has a heavy base.

MARBLES AND GLASS

Especially in clear glass containers, marbles help to hide the stems of plant material, and in any type of container give weight and stability to the arrangement. Crushed or broken glass from automobile windows can be used in the same way as marbles. Because it looks like water, such glass can be used combined with aquatic plants to enhance the water effect. Broken *windshield* glass is not suitable.

PLASTER AND POLYFILLER

Anything you anchor with plaster or polyfiller is there permanently because they set hard and hold dried-plant material securely. They also set quickly, so before you begin, know exactly what you are going to do, and then work fast. You can rub the hard dried surface with shoe polish to change its color. Plaster and polyfiller are especially effective when large, awkward, or heavy branches need to be held in place.

WIRE NETTING

Crumpled chicken wire has long been used by flower arrangers to hold flowers in position. Wearing sturdy work gloves, press it into a mass with your hands. A pliable, and more durable, plastic-coated netting is now available. Though either of them can be used alone in a heavy container, they are more often combined with sand or floral foam for best effect. When it is balled up, the cut ends of either material can be used to twist around individual stems to give them extra support. These ends can often be hitched to the container itself, too. If you use chicken wire, you will find that the larger meshes are more flexible than the fine-meshed ones.

PINHOLDERS

If you are using a heavy lead-based pinholder alone, first fix it firmly with floral clay to the base or container you are going to use. Plastic pinholders should be glued to the base or container, all of which should then be weighed down.

When using pinholders it is often necessary to put sand or grit underneath to raise the holder to the required height. Weight is also added in this way. A piece of floral foam can even be speared onto a pinholder and then the dried material arranged in a container that has thus been stabilized. Either wire netting or plastic-coated netting can be used to make a cage over a pinholder, which will give you even greater arrangement possibilities.

Sometimes a branch will sit better if a short piece of hollow stem is placed on the pinholder and then the plant branch inserted into it (Figure 13).

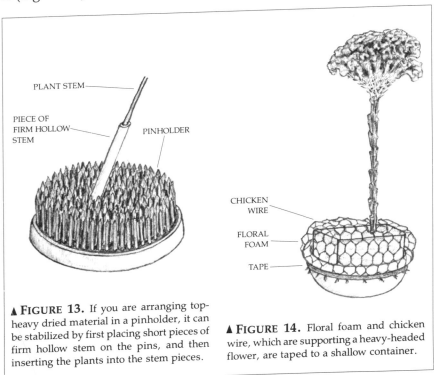

PLANT STEM

PIECE OF FIRM HOLLOW STEM

PINHOLDER

CHICKEN WIRE

FLORAL FOAM

TAPE

▲ **FIGURE 13.** If you are arranging top-heavy dried material in a pinholder, it can be stabilized by first placing short pieces of firm hollow stem on the pins, and then inserting the plants into the stem pieces.

▲ **FIGURE 14.** Floral foam and chicken wire, which are supporting a heavy-headed flower, are taped to a shallow container.

POSSIBLE COMBINATIONS OF THE ABOVE MECHANICS

When using a deep container for large arrangements, wire netting can be crumpled and put onto sand. Thus the stems are positioned by the netting and held below by the sand. Sand alone will not hold the stems firmly in place because it tends to shift.

To secure heavy plant material in a shallow container, wire netting should be placed over foam (preferably Ultra Foam), both of which are then secured to the container with medical adhesive tape. This method gives good support to heavy plant stems (Figure 14).

Plumber's lead, which is heavy, can be shaped into small rings to support individual stems. It should be anchored in place with floral clay and is a great help when making Oriental-style arrangements.

Do not hesitate to use any combination of these mechanics if they will keep your container stable and the stems secured in the position you prefer. In this regard, you will find that Sahara and/or Ultra Foam will give you the most flexibility for the least cost.

Designs *can* be made without any of these mechanics, but the scope of these designs will be limited. Simple posies, bouquets, and hanging bunches are particularly pleasing. For more on such designs, see the chapter entitled "Projects Using Unpressed Dried-Plant Material."

USING FRESH AND DRIED-PLANT MATERIAL TOGETHER

If you want to place a few fresh flowers in an arrangement of predominantly dried material, you can put them in florist's tubes, plastic pill containers, test tubes, cigar tubes, or orchid tubes. Fill the tubes with water and secure them in whatever mechanics you are using for the dried-plant material.

If you want the dried arrangement to be permanent, you must be able to change the water and renew the fresh flowers without disturbing it. To do this, tape the water-holding tubes to sticks or bamboo canes; then you will be able to remove and replace them easily.

On the other hand, if your fresh flowers are going to be grouped together, secure a small water-holding container for them *inside* a bigger container. Arrange the dried material in this bigger container and you will have no problem keeping it dry.

Contrariwise, when you want to put some dried-plant material into an arrangement of fresh flowers, put it into tubes that are filled with dry foam. Then push these tubes into the mechanics you are using for the fresh flowers or tape them to a cane or stick as before. Any small individually dried flowers whose stems are short should be taped to florist's picks, so that when you insert them into water or wet foam the dried flowers will not get wet.

A method about which I have recently heard, but not yet tried, is to anchor Oasis (wet foam) in a container and then secure a piece of

Sahara (dry foam) on top of it. To do this push two wires through both pieces of foam. Fresh-flower stems are pushed into the wet foam and the dried material into the Sahara. The Sahara will not absorb the moisture from the wet foam underneath it.

In a predominantly fresh arrangement you can also use heavy leafy stems or branches that have been preserved in glycerine if you first dip a few inches of the stems into melted canning wax or bind them with a waterproof tape. Either method will prevent the stems from absorbing water.

WORKING WITH DRIED-PLANT MATERIAL
SOME DOS & DON'TS

DO work in warm dry atmosphere and **DON'T** expose plant material to dampness while you are working on it.

DON'T work where the sun shines on the dried plants.

DON'T work under fluorescent lights—incandescent light or daylight only.

DO take the time and trouble to store your dried-plant material properly.

DO be sure that all plant material to be stored is in perfect condition.

DON'T store plant material that shows signs of mildew.

DO label all storage boxes and tins clearly with the name of the plant material and the date it was put in storage.

DO label stacked boxes on the sides, not the tops: you will then be able to find what you are looking for much more easily.

DO remember that packing material in shallow boxes is less likely to damage it than packing it several layers deep.

DON'T crowd the storage boxes with too many plants.

DO support flower heads.

DO use silica gel in all storage boxes, especially those that are not airtight. This will prevent the dried-plant material from reabsorbing moisture from the air.

DO put paper towels between the silica gel and the dried-plant material, or put the silica gel in cotton bags and put these in the storage boxes.

DO reactivate the silica gel (by drying it in the oven) as soon as it starts to turn from blue to pink or white.

WIRING
& MAKING FALSE STEMS

W IRING IS BEST USED:

- ❧ When natural stems need replacing or reinforcing because they are not thick enough or tough enough to withstand handling, or if they are not strong enough to support the flower heads.
- ❧ To enable stems to hold a curve.
- ❧ When the natural stem has to be cut short to dry the flower in a desiccant. Then either a short wire stem is made, which is easily lengthened later, or a long wire stem can be made and bent so that it will fit in the box of desiccant. Such bendable stems will also simplify storage of the dried materials later.
- ❧ When stems need to be lengthened.

FLORIST'S WIRE

Florist's wire comes in many thicknesses, but the lower the gauge number the thicker the wire. The thickness of the wire required will depend on the type, size, and weight of the flower heads or plant material that is being wired. A good rule to follow is that the wire should be firm enough to pierce fresh green plant material without undue pressure. If you want to bend the stems so they look natural, do not choose wire that is too thick. Wire can be bought in many different lengths, but it is usually more economical to buy it in the longest length available, so you can cut it into shorter lengths as necessary.

You will probably use gauges 20, 22, and 24 more than any others for wiring flowers and leaves. Gauge 34 is the finest rose or reel wire (sometimes called paddle wire), and it is used to bind light material together or to make garlands and wreaths. Tiny bell-shaped florets (hyacinths, bluebells, and lily-of-the-valley, for example) can be threaded on it like beads.

Most plant material should be wired while it is still fresh. However, do not dry wired plants in a microwave—any type of metal and microwaves don't mix. Leaves should also be dried or preserved, in glycerine, before wiring.

To prevent unused wire from rusting in storage keep it in an oiled and closed polyethylene bag. If you need to *stick* wire to a natural stem use china cement.

FLOWERS WITH SHORT THICK STEMS

While the sap is still in the stems, insert the wire through the stem and just into the head of the flower. Be careful not to penetrate the flower head completely because the wire could damage it. The sap will cause the wire to corrode and this corrosion, and the shrinkage caused by the drying of the plant material, will ensure that the wire stays firmly in the flower head.

Wiring in this way is recommended for globe amaranths (*Gomphrena globosa*), strawflowers (*Helichrysum bracteatum*), and some of the thicker-stemmed daisies. Plastic-coated wire will not corrode and is very smooth, so it is not suitable for these kinds of flowers.

FLOWERS WITH A THICK BASE OR CALYX

Cut two wires about 6 inches (15 cm) long and push them through the base of the flower at right angles to each other. Bend down the ends and twist them together (Figure 15). This will make a stem 3 inches (7.5 cm) long that can be lengthened later if necessary.

DAISY-TYPE FLOWERS

You can wire many of the daisy-type flowers the same as those with a thick base or calyx, but use one wire instead of two, bend it down on each side of the stem, twist the two ends together, and cover the wire with tape.

There is a method called hairpin wiring that is often recommended, but it is, my opinion, unnecessarily time consuming and can damage the flower even when done with great care. Nonetheless, here is the

▲ FIGURE 15. To wire flowers with a thick calyx, cut off the stem just below the calyx and push two 6-inch pieces of wire through it at right angles (left). Bend down the wire and twist it together to create a short wire stem (right).

◄ FIGURE 16. Position of the hooked wire when hairpin wiring is used.

procedure. Leave about one-half inch (approximately 1.5 cm) of stem on the flower. Make a hook one-quarter inch (.5 cm) long at one end of the wire, push the unhooked end through the center of the flower, and pull it downwards. If the stem is hollow push the wire through it, but if it is not, direct the wire alongside the piece of natural stem that is left and use tape to cover it (Figure 16). The hook should be pulled down far enough into the flower to be hidden, but be careful not to damage it.

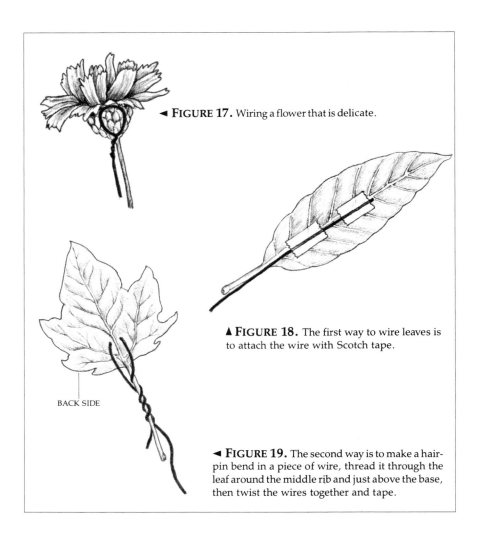

◄ **FIGURE 17.** Wiring a flower that is delicate.

▲ **FIGURE 18.** The first way to wire leaves is to attach the wire with Scotch tape.

BACK SIDE

◄ **FIGURE 19.** The second way is to make a hair-pin bend in a piece of wire, thread it through the leaf around the middle rib and just above the base, then twist the wires together and tape.

FLOWERS THAT ARE DELICATE

After they have been dried, delicate flower heads will sometimes shatter or disintegrate when an attempt is made to wire them by one of the other methods. To reinforce the natural stems of such flowers, make a loop at one end of the wire and place it up under the flower head. Keeping the wire parallel to the natural stem, tape them together (Figure 17).

LEAVES

Use the lightest wire that will take the weight of the leaf and still be able to support it. There are three different ways to wire leaves. The first method is to lay the wire along the middle rib on the back of the leaf and attach it with Scotch tape in two or three places (Figure 18). The second is to make a hairpin bend just off center on a piece of wire. Thread one end through the leaf behind the middle rib and just above its base. Then twist the wire together and tape it (Figure 19). And the last method is for leaves that have only short pieces of natural stem. Pierce the leaf just above its base, double the wire downwards, and twist it together (Figure 20). A number of leaves mounted like this can be formed into a spray by then mounting them onto a heavier wire (Figure 21).

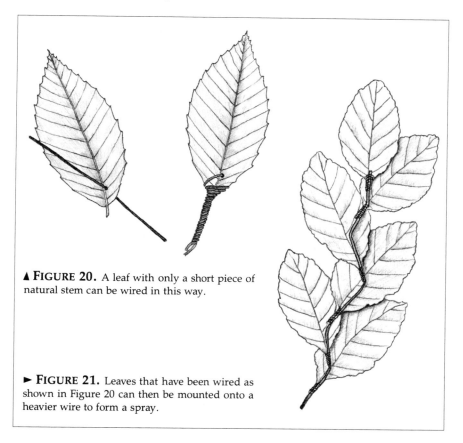

▲ **FIGURE 20.** A leaf with only a short piece of natural stem can be wired in this way.

▶ **FIGURE 21.** Leaves that have been wired as shown in Figure 20 can then be mounted onto a heavier wire to form a spray.

WHEN NATURAL STEMS NEED REINFORCING

If the stem is not hollow, insert the wire just below the flower head and push it gently, but firmly, upwards. Stop before it completely penetrates the flower head. Twist the wire round the stem (never try to twist the stem round the wire), and keeping the wire flat against the stem, twist it in a long gentle spiral, *not* a tight spiral like a spring (Figure 22).

With some stems it is possible to push the wire through the center of the stem into the flower head, being careful to stop before it penetrates completely; it must not show. Everlasting sand flowers (*Ammobium alatum*) can be wired in this way. If neither of these methods is practical, the wire may be laid along the flower stem so that one end is well up under the flower head. The stem and wire are then taped together. This method is good for heavy-headed flowers, such as globe artichokes and some eryngos.

BUNCHES OF TINY FLOWER HEADS

As long as tiny flower heads have some stem, little bunches can be wired together with fine reel wire. Thicker wire is then twisted around that bunch, enough being left over to form a "stem" (Figure 23). All the wire should be covered with tape. The flowers of pearly everlasting (*Anaphalis margaritacea*) can be bunched and wired like this, for example.

LENGTHENING SHORT STEMS WITH WIRE

When a flexible false stem is needed, wire can be used to lengthen a natural or wire stem that is too short. Choose a wire of suitable length and comparable thickness to serve as a new false stem. Using fine reel wire, bind the wire stem to the existing short stem, and tape them together from top to bottom. Or as shown in Figure 15, you can insert wire through the flower's calyx, bend it down, twist the wire together, and tape it.

▲ **FIGURE 22.** To reinforce natural stems that are not hollow, push a piece of wire upward into the flower head or calyx, but do not let it completely penetrate. Then carefully twist the wire around the stem in a gentle spiral.

▲ **FIGURE 23.** Create a bunch of small flower heads by wiring them with fine wire. Then twist a thicker piece of wire around the bunch with a bit left over, if necessary, to form a stem. All the wire should be taped.

COLLECT STRONG NATURAL STEMS

Throughout the growing season collect stiff strong stems from plants of every sort and size, remove the flowers or blooms, and dry them. Goldenrods (*Solidago* spp) and yarrows (*Achillea* spp) are two examples of plants with useful stems. They can be used to lengthen or reinforce stems and flower heads by some of the methods described in the section that follows, or they can be stuck with hot wax to the original flower stems.

USING HOLLOW STEMS

Throughout the summer and early fall collect and dry a variety of hollow stems, which will later serve many purposes. Most members of the Umbelliferae family (angelica, dill, fennel, lovage, and Queen-Anne's-lace are just a few) have hollow stems and so do many grasses and grains.

A flower that has only a short piece of its own stem can be lengthened by dropping it into a section of hollow stem (Figure 24). If it seems at all insecure, anchor it with a spot of glue.

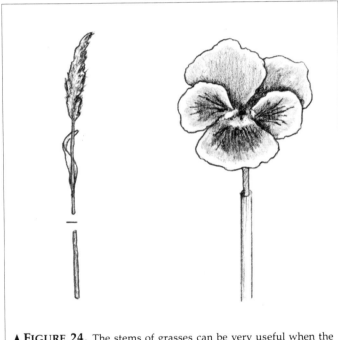

▲ **FIGURE 24.** The stems of grasses can be very useful when the tops are cut off and they are dried (left). You can lengthen a short flower stem by placing it in a section of hollow plant stem (right).

It is often necessary to remove most of the natural stem of a flower that must be dried in a desiccant. Sometimes it is possible to dry that stem separately and rejoin it later to the dried flower head. To do this, insert a short piece of wire into the flower head before drying. A hole needs to be made in the stem (unless it is hollow) while it is drying, which can be done by sticking in a safety pin, a short length of plastic-covered wire, or a toothpick. All are easy to remove after drying. When all the materials are dry, the wire in the flower head can be pushed into the hole in the stem. Several flower heads, each with fine wire stems, can be bunched then pushed together into a large hollow stem (Figure 25); a little bouquet can be made in this way.

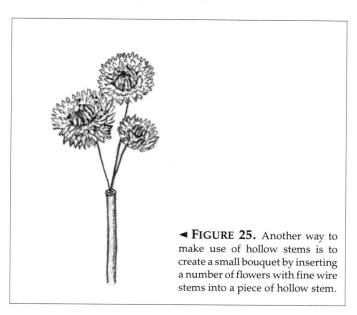

◄ **FIGURE 25.** Another way to make use of hollow stems is to create a small bouquet by inserting a number of flowers with fine wire stems into a piece of hollow stem.

Any flower with a long wire stem can be dropped into a hollow false stem to conceal the wire; strawflowers (*Helichrysum bracteatum*) can be prepared in this way. Plants with weak natural stems, such as acrocliniums (*Helipterum roseum*), can be treated the same, though drinking straws make better false stems for delicate flowers such as these. Use a neutral color or pale green straw—it will look more natural.

If you have a flower head that has a wide hollow stem, your false stem does not also need to be hollow—it should be *smaller* in diameter. Cut the original stem about 2 inches (5 cm) long and push the false stem up into it; anchor it with glue, if necessary. This method works well for giant sea holly (*Eryngium giganteum*).

Some advice: when making an arrangement you will find that it is easier to *first* push the false hollow stems or straws into your anchoring material and *then* drop the flower into the hollow stem or straw.

TAPING

It is always necessary to conceal wires and joins, so unless you are going to hide these inside hollow stems as already described, bind them with floral tape. This is a stretchable colored tape that is wound spirally around the wire and/or join.

If you are right-handed hold one end of the tape on the stem, up against the base of the flower with your left hand; press the tape firmly against the flower base with your thumb and index finger. Hold the roll of tape in your right hand. Turn the stem, spinning it slowly with your left hand so that the tape covers the wire in *overlapping* spirals (Figure 26). Move your left hand down the stem as you tape to keep

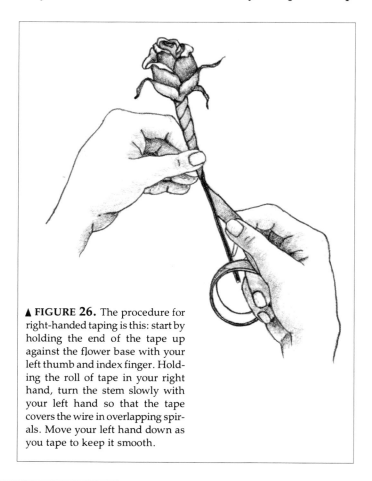

▲ **FIGURE 26.** The procedure for right-handed taping is this: start by holding the end of the tape up against the flower base with your left thumb and index finger. Holding the roll of tape in your right hand, turn the stem slowly with your left hand so that the tape covers the wire in overlapping spirals. Move your left hand down as you tape to keep it smooth.

it smooth. If you are left-handed hold the tape against the flower base and then along the stem with your right hand and hold the roll of tape with your left hand.

You can tape several flowers to create a staggered spike (Figure 27) by adding a flower at a time as you twist the tape around the stem, which may be either false or natural.

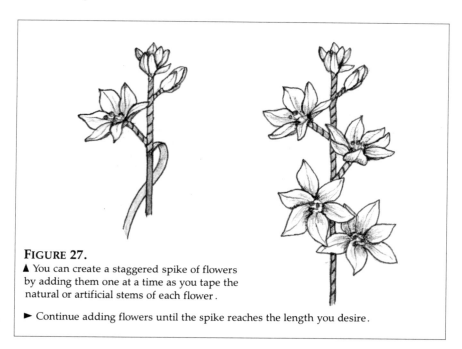

FIGURE 27.
▲ You can create a staggered spike of flowers by adding them one at a time as you tape the natural or artificial stems of each flower.

▶ Continue adding flowers until the spike reaches the length you desire.

Be sure to exert pressure on the tape as it is spiraled down the stem, and don't cover it to the very end—bare wire is easier to insert into foam. Don't expect perfect results until you have had a little practice: taping isn't the easiest thing to learn!

PROJECTS
USING UNPRESSED
DRIED-PLANT MATERIAL

UNPRESSED DRIED-PLANT MATERIAL can be used in so many crafts and projects. Those described in this section are to help you get started. Give your imagination free rein—it may only be limited by your manual dexterity.

ABOUT ARRANGEMENTS

The object of this book is to help you to grow, dry, preserve, and use all kinds of dried-plant material, not teach you the theory of floral design and arrangement. The book would, however, be incomplete without some mention of the different kinds of arrangements that can be made. I am not going to attempt to tell you what is acceptable or not acceptable when designing an arrangement because I'm not a skilled artistic flower arranger myself. I tend toward the "let's-put-another-flower-in-there-and-see-how-it-looks" school.

Creating original arrangements with dried-plant material is often a lot easier than it is with fresh flowers. The season for specific fresh flowers is often short, whereas with plenty of dried material in storage, one is not restricted by what is currently in season. Modern mechanics and the use of unconventional containers enable you to position plant material at angles that would be impossible if it needed to be in water.

The first thing to consider is where you want to place your arrangement. If it will be against a wall, the front and side views are the most important and the back can be flat. If it will be a table centerpiece then keep it low and view it from all sides as you make it; remember that it will be seen from all angles when complete.

A posy can be slipped as it is into a narrow-necked container; put it on a low table where it can be viewed from above. Massed arrangements of the Colonial type, or those based on a painting by an old Dutch master, need a big room to show them off to the best advantage. Arrangements in the Japanese form can be made with a few well-chosen pieces of material in flat dishes, on trays, or in narrow-necked bottles or vases. If you are making miniature arrangements, the most important thing to remember is to maintain the appropriate proportion between the container and the material.

If you prefer your dried plants to look natural and unarranged, you can't go wrong with a basket as a container. They come in so many shapes and sizes and accentuate the natural look and warm fall colors of many dried flowers.

THREE-DIMENSIONAL FLOWER & LEAF PICTURES

Three-dimensional flower pictures are put together in a way different from pictures made from pressed flowers and leaves. They are assembled much like a plaque. Then they are framed. Before you start making your design with dried plants, get the frame ready. You will need a box frame that has at least one-half inch (1.25 cm) of space, but preferably 1 inch (2.5 cm), between the glass and the back of the frame (Figure 28A). Suitable old frames can often be found in antique and second-hand stores or thrift shops. You may be lucky enough to find a shadow box (a shallow enclosing case usually with a glass front) or you can make a box frame by building a small shallow box and attaching it to the back of an ordinary frame (Figures 28B and 28C). Sometimes, depending on the depth of the frame, enough extra space can be made by fixing narrow wooden molding (or beading) behind the frame. If you experience any difficulties putting together such a frame according to the directions that follow, consult a handyman for advice and assistance.

Glue the glass to the frame to keep out dust and moisture. Cut a back board to fit the back opening of the frame, and cover it in the same way as when making a pressed-flower picture (Figure 28D).

Then make your three-dimensional flower picture on this covered back board. Put glue on the edges of the back of the frame, and then put the picture in place (Figure 28E). Cover the back of the frame with stiff paper or cardboard and seal it with waterproof tape. There will be a space between the dried-plant material and the glass, so be sure to use ordinary glass, *not* the nonglare type because it would cause unwanted reflections.

In a book that was published in 1965, but is now out of print (*Creative Decorations With Dried Flowers* by Dorothy Thompson), some photographs of three-dimensional flower pictures in shadow boxes were shown, and those shadow boxes were made from sardine cans. It seems to me that if sardine cans are acceptable, then oval fish cans and ham cans could also be used! Baking soda will get rid of the fish (and other) smells. Dissolve about 2 teaspoons of baking soda in one quart of water and soak the can in this solution for a few hours; rinse and wash with regular dish detergent.

I have seen some attractive arrangements that look as though they are "pouring" themselves out of a picture frame. As pleasing as this style is, just remember that unless the plant material is kept airtight, it will not last forever.

A friend of ours has a beautiful three-dimensional flower picture covered with a convex glass. It is almost forty years old now and the colors are still true to life. Of course, it has always been kept airtight and out of the sunlight.

ARTICLES TO WEAR OR TO HOLD

CORSAGES of dried flowers are made in the same way you would make them with fresh flowers. Wire and tape each stem, then arrange the material in one hand and fasten the stems together, as you go, with fine wire. Suitable dried materials can always be found to fit any occasion, and one of the great advantages of making corsages with dried flowers is that they can be made ahead of time.

GARLANDS for the hair are made in a manner similar to that for corsages—each flower stem being wired and well taped. They are put together in two identical half circles, which are then bound

FIGURE 28. A THREE-DIMENSIONAL FLOWER PICTURE

A

B

BOX FRAME
COMPONENTS

C

ASSEMBLED
BOX FRAME

D

BACK BOARD
COVERING

BACK BOARD

BOX
FRAME

PICTURE
FRAME

ASSEMBLED THREE-DIMENSIONAL
FLOWER PICTURE

together so that a circlet is formed to fit the head of the wearer. I have seen it suggested that nylon stockings can be twisted into a rope, then the flower steams either poked through the stockings or bound to them with raffia, but I have never tried this method (insecure flowers could be spot stuck with glue to the stockings). In the same way, stretchy athletic headbands could be used as a base. The Beckers of Goodwin Creek Gardens (see the Appendix for a list of Sources) make garlands of strawflowers and ribbons, which are charming on a girl's straw hat.

BOUQUETS of dried flowers are made in a similar way to corsages. The stems are wired and taped individually, then the whole bunch taped or wired together in whatever form you wish. A bow of ribbon can be used to give a finished appearance to bouquets.

Fresh-flower bouquets can sometimes be entirely preserved in silica gel. If this is not practical because of their form, they should be taken apart, the flowers dried individually in silica gel, and then reassembled.

POSIES are similar to bouquets, though they are usually smaller and round in form. Start by binding a few flowers together with fine wire, turning the bunch as you add more and more flowers until a well-spaced round bunch is formed (Figure 29). It is usually not

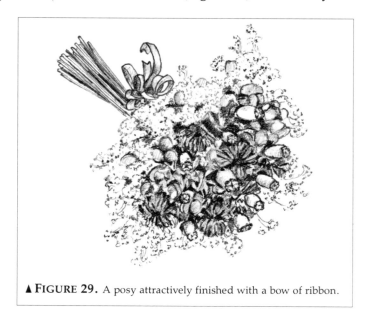

▲ **FIGURE 29.** A posy attractively finished with a bow of ribbon.

necessary to wire and tape individual stems, except for brittle ones such as strawflowers.

You can also make a very attractive quick posy by using a plastic bouquet holder with a foam center (available at craft shops) into which you push flower stems. Attractive lacy collars can be bought that are attached to a cup-shaped piece of plastic with a hole in the middle. The flower stem or the handle of the bouquet holder can be pushed through this hole, securing the lacy collar around the bouquet.

TUSSIE MUSSIES are attractive little nosegays of herbs or herbs and flowers. They can be made of fresh material and hung to dry or can be made of dried material. Originally they were carried by judges in the eighteenth-century England to ward off the smells in their courts!

On Valentine's Day they can be made to express special sentiments depending on which flowers are chosen. Often a rosebud is put at the center, surrounded by a few gray-green leaves, such as *Santolina*, a few sprigs of rosemary, and so on. Tussie mussies can be inserted into a lacy collar, like a posy to finish them off attractively.

FREESTANDING DECORATIONS

CANDELABRA can be used to hold dried flowers with the help of candlecups inserted into each of the candle holes. A candle cup is shown in Figure 10. If your arrangement will be fairly large, only use one branch of the candelabrum. If you want to decorate more than one branch, candle wreaths (below) would probably be more effective.

CANDLE WREATHS can be made by cutting a hole in the center of a circular piece of Styrofoam or Ultra Foam that is the diameter of the candle you have chosen to use. Then push the candle into this hole, being sure that a half inch (1.5 cm) goes through the foam and out of the other side. Now arrange the dried flowers in the foam and then push the candle into the candle holder. Need I say don't light the candle amongst all that dry material?

FLOWER AND CONE TREES are simple to make with Styrofoam, which is available in a variety of shapes and sizes. For instance, a ball can be pushed onto a piece of dowel, secured at its base, then covered with flower heads. To do this, small holes should be made in the Styrofoam with a coarse sewing needle or fine knitting needle (depending on the thickness of the stems to be inserted). It is not usually necessary to wire the flowers. The end of the dowel must be anchored in a pot or tub filled with plaster of paris or polyfiller, either of which can be stained with shoe polish or covered with pebbles when dry.

Alternatively, a cone-shaped piece of Styrofoam can be glued to a suitable base (a pedestal shape is attractive) and covered with flower heads. Attractive Christmas decorations are made in this way using cones from coniferous trees instead of flowers.

HANGING ITEMS

GARLIC BRAIDS to hang in the kitchen can be made much more attractive if you thread fresh flowers that air dry well into the braid as you make it. The garlic is likely to be ready to lift from the garden at about the same time you would harvest many of the true everlastings described in Part I. This idea was suggested to me by Heidi Clift of Mountain View, Missouri; she grows everlasting flowers commercially. I see that Goodwin Creek Gardens of Williams, Oregon, sells braids of their organically grown garlic, which have about fourteen to sixteen heads threaded with their own everlasting flowers.

HANGING BUNCHES of drying or dried flowers can add color to any room, whether they are all of one variety or a mixture of carefully selected colors and varieties chosen to complement the area in which they are hung. They will be viewed from below, so bear this in mind when you put them together. Taping and wiring is seldom needed. Don't hang them in direct sunlight or where they can get greasy—the colors may fade or the dried plants could be soiled and damaged.

WALL VASES that you hesitate to use with fresh flowers for fear of dripping water, are ideal for dried-plant material. Use Sahara or Ultra Foam in the wall vase to secure the stems. An attractive wall vase can be made by splitting a lotus pod in half. Attach it to a board with glue and you will have a wall panel or plaque. The

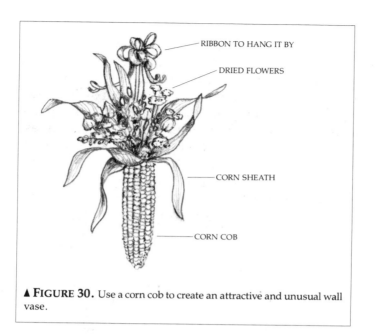

RIBBON TO HANG IT BY

DRIED FLOWERS

CORN SHEATH

CORN COB

▲ **FIGURE 30.** Use a corn cob to create an attractive and unusual wall vase.

holes in the pod can be filled with dried-plant material. Or use a corn cob as shown in Figure 30.

A PLAQUE OR WALL PANEL is defined as a design of materials permanently assembled together on a visible background with dried-plant materials dominating. This is slightly different from a swag, which is a collection of materials assembled *without* a visible background, plant materials being dominant.

It is hardly worthwhile making bases for plaques because there are so many inexpensive and readily available items that you can use. Table mats made of bamboo, cork, raffia, straw, or wood are all suitable; cheese and bread boards, too. Weathered wood and shingles from razed buildings or old fences often have a beautiful sheen. A visit to a lumberyard will give you some idea as to the enormous variety of grains, colors, and textures of the different woods that are available. Rectangular pieces measuring 10-by-20 inches (25-by-50 cm) are a suitable size for the base of a small plaque. You can, or course, make the base larger, but keep the proportion of height to width about the same.

You may need to give some of these pieces of wood two or three *thin* coats of shellac, varnish, or wax to create a pleasing finish.

Or the base can be covered with fabric, coarse linen, sacking, canvas, or even netting. When the base has been prepared choose your plant material. Flowers and leaves, grasses, berries, nuts, gourds, seedpods, and cones can all be used. Do not glue anything until you have completed the design to your satisfaction. Then use a toothpick to apply the glue in small amounts to the back of the material; press it firmly and gently in place. Unless you're using fast drying glue, leave the plaque flat for a few days to give the glue time to harden.

SWAGS are distinguished from a plaque or wall panel by the fact that the base or background is not visible. They can, of course, be made without any base at all, using a background of grass or grain or other tall dried-plant material. Similar to a hanging bunch, but more compact, swags must be flat backed in order to lie against the wall or door on which they are hung.

If you want to make a swag with a base, use Sahara or Ultra Foam. If you can get sheets of either of these foams, cut a piece to the size and shape you want. Try using round and oval bases as well as the typical rectangular shapes. If you can't get *sheets* of the floral foam, standard bricks can be wired (using heavy floral wire) together to create a long narrow base (Figure 31). When cutting and wiring the foam remember to make a wire loop to hang it by. The easiest way to make a swag is to buy blocks of foam fixed to a plastic board, complete with a loop, and ready to use.

Push the longest-stemmed plant material into the foam *first*, work from the center up or down or start at either end and work toward the center, and *then* fill in any gaps with shorter-stemmed material. This is the way to avoid damage to your materials. When you have finished, the base should not show at all.

Swags can also be made using a thin "roll" of chicken wire filled with moss, as shown in Figure 32.

GARLANDS are made in rope form to be hung or draped. Dried-plant material is secured with fine wire or raffia to a doubled piece of rope (the thickness of a clothesline is about right). If it is to be hung, a loop, where the rope is doubled, is left free of plant material. If it is to be draped over a mantel or bookcase, plant material covers the rope from top to bottom.

To keep the rope steady while you work, secure a hook at a convenient height, and loop the rope over it. More delicate garlands

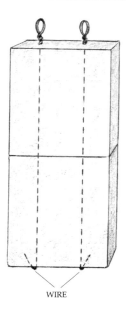

WIRE

◄ FIGURE 31. To make a swag with bricks of floral foam push two long pieces of heavy wire through two bricks of foam and push the bricks together. At one end, turn the wire up to form a hook, give the bricks another push for reinforcement, and at the other end, bend the wire into loops so that the finished swag can be hung.

▼ FIGURE 32. Make a swag with chicken wire. A) Roll a width of chicken wire into a narrow cylinder and fill it with dried moss. B) Cover the back with a strip of green felt and attach a loop to hang it by. C) Fill it in with dried flowers and plants; a pleasing finished dimension is 6 inches wide by 17 or 18 inches long.

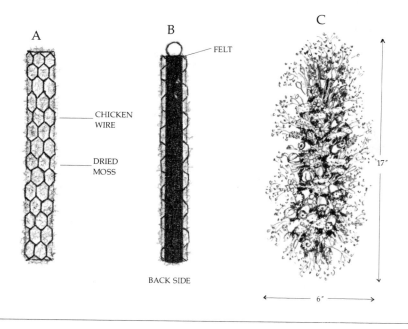

A

CHICKEN WIRE

DRIED MOSS

B

FELT

BACK SIDE

C

17˝

6˝

can be made using a thinner rope or thick string, but let me warn you, this requires a greater degree of manual dexterity.

WREATHS were once synonymous with Christmas and funerals and usually purchased from a florist. With the availability of ready-made bases and other mechanics, and the popularity of dried flower and plant material, even the least artistic of us can make attractive wreaths with a minimum of time and trouble.

You can choose from a number of different materials that will all serve as bases for a wreath. Bases made of Styrofoam are available in a variety of sizes or you can cut your own from sheets of Ultra Foam. You can buy rigid wire frames at a craft shop, make your own from old wire coat hangers, or wire lamp shade rings. They can be round, oval, or heart shaped, but wire frames will have to be padded with dry moss first. You can buy grapevines twisted into a circle. If you are lucky enough to have a honey-suckle vine which bends and twists well, old tendrils can be twisted to form a wreath. Straw wreath bases can be bought or you can plait your own with raffia.

Although you can push wired or strong natural stems into foam, straw, or raffia, or wire them to the wire frames and vines, it is much quicker to use a glue gun. Sometimes you may have to use U-shaped wire pins, especially when making Christmas wreaths because of the ornaments.

The Pleasure of Herbs by Phyllis V. Shaudys (Garden Way Publishing, 1986) has a number of wreath designs for special occasions, many original ideas for Christmas decorations, and instructions on how to make them.

KISSING BALLS are a simple modern version of the old-fashioned, elaborately made kissing ring. Traditionally a Christmas decoration, it can be made with any combination of dried flowers.

You will need a Styrofoam ball about 5 inches (12.5 cm) in diameter and one (or more) smaller-sized balls. The balls must then be completely covered with flowers. You can either push the stems into holes made in the Styrofoam with a coarse needle or you can stick the flowers on with glue. The balls are then hung by a cord or ribbons threaded through their center. You can add more balls—the number will depend on how much head room there is where it will hang. Be sure that the smallest ball is at the top and the largest at the bottom.

OTHER LITTLE THINGS

TINY CORSAGE-LIKE ARRANGEMENTS can add charm to any gift-wrapped package. They can either be made like an ordinary corsage (except smaller) or the flowers can be pushed into or stuck onto a tiny piece of foam. This small arrangement is then glued to the package. A piece cut from a foam tray on which meat is packed can be used if you are gluing the flowers; most plant stems are not sturdy enough to push through this type of foam.

TO GIVE EXTRA COLOR TO YOUR POTPOURRIS, bright-colored dried flower petals can be added. They don't have to have any perfume, just color.

Today I read this item in our newspaper: "The world's first **SCENTED TELEPHONE**. Hitachi's Populene features a plastic mouthpiece capsule containing dried flowers. Smelling of roses and lavender, the push-button phone comes with five tunes to serenade callers on hold, plus a 20-number memory storage."

LAVENDER DOLLIES, sometimes called lavender sticks, wands, or bottles, are made with freshly harvested lavender stems. You can use them wherever you want the lavender scent, but they are especially lovely when used in the places where you store bed linens or towels. Pick the stems when a few of the blossoms have begun to open. Each dolly will need an odd number of stems, so start with thirteen. Follow these directions and Figure 33 for guidance.

1) Strip off any odd blooms at the lower end of each stem to make a compact flower head.
2) Cut a length of ribbon 3/8 inch (1 cm) wide, 45 inches (1.2 m) long.
3) Knot the ribbon just below the bunch of flower heads so that the short end is about 12 inches (30 cm) long.
4) Hold the bunch of lavender in one hand, stems up and blossoms down. Let the short end of the ribbon hang down, too.
5) With the other hand bend the stems at the knot, so they are turned down over the flower heads and the short end of the ribbon.
6) With the long strand of ribbon, weave over and under the stems, pulling the ribbon quite tight with a toothpick as you go. The short piece is left to hang. Continue weaving until the flower heads are all covered.

7) The flower stems will shrink while drying, so put off finishing the dolly until it has dried for a week or ten days. Hang it in a cool dry place with good air circulation.
8) Tighten the ribbons with a toothpick if they are at all slack after drying and tie the two ends in a tight bow.
9) For a variation, try using more than thirteen stems (but always use an odd number). You can use different widths and different kinds of ribbon. If you are feeling extravagant, try making one with a velvet ribbon, but get a little experience with other less expensive kinds first! The maximum manageable number of stems to use is about nineteen. In time the dolly may seem to be losing its fragrance. Just rub it gently between the palms of your hands and it will all come back.

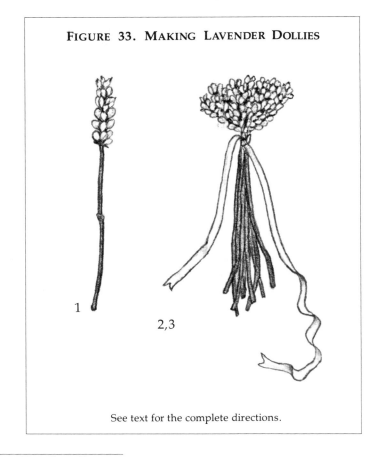

FIGURE 33. MAKING LAVENDER DOLLIES

1

2,3

See text for the complete directions.

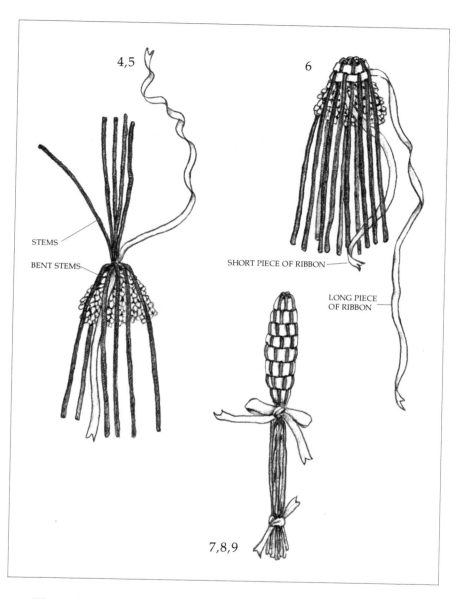

4,5

6

STEMS

BENT STEMS

SHORT PIECE OF RIBBON

LONG PIECE
OF RIBBON

7,8,9

These directions are based on the illustrated instruction sheet for making traditional English lavender dollies, which can be obtained from Goodwin Creek Gardens. The instructions given here are from that sheet and are used with the kind permission of Jim and Dotti Becker.

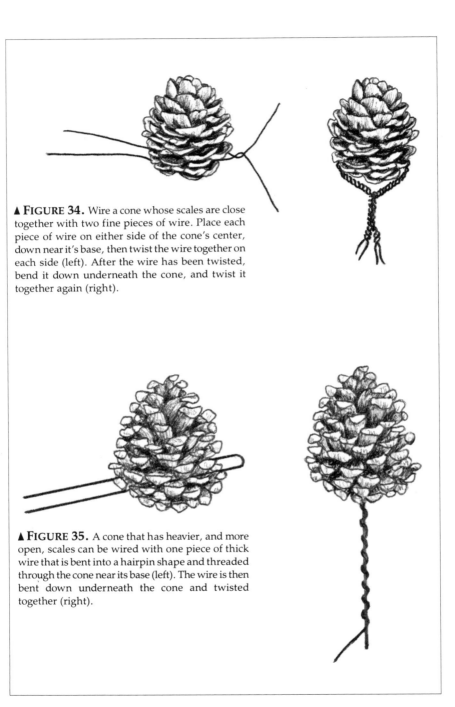

▲ FIGURE 34. Wire a cone whose scales are close together with two fine pieces of wire. Place each piece of wire on either side of the cone's center, down near it's base, then twist the wire together on each side (left). After the wire has been twisted, bend it down underneath the cone, and twist it together again (right).

▲ FIGURE 35. A cone that has heavier, and more open, scales can be wired with one piece of thick wire that is bent into a hairpin shape and threaded through the cone near its base (left). The wire is then bent down underneath the cone and twisted together (right).

A Christmas Reminder

Many of the things you can make with dried-plant material that have been described in this section, can be adapted for special occasions. White flowers offset the bright reds and greens traditionally used to decorate at Christmas. One is inclined to forget how many everlastings are white. Baby's-breath (*Gypsophila paniculata*), everlasting sand flower (*Ammobium alatum*), and pearly everlasting (*Anaphalis margaritacea*) are white. There are white acrocliniums (*Helipterum roseum*), immortelles (*Xeranthemum annuum*), and statice (*Limonium sinuatum*). Don't forget the silvery pods of honesty (*Lunaria annua*) and starflower (*Scabiosa stellata*) can be sprayed white or any other color you choose.

You can use microwave-dried or glycerine-preserved leaves and, of course, dried cones of any shape or size. Cones are especially useful in Christmas projects, but you will often need to wire them so that they can be secured in place. Figure 34 shows two fine wires being used on a cone whose scales are close together; this method gives you a strong "stem" with four thicknesses of wire. Figure 35 shows a heavier cone with more open scales for which you can use one thicker piece of wire that is bent down and twisted to form a stem.

Designing "Flowers" Such as Nature Never Intended

Artificial flowers of all kinds, even unquestionably beautiful silk flowers, are anathema to me. But "flowers" that are made entirely from dried, natural plant material are another matter. They can look quite beautiful, though I have seen some tortured specimens that were positively bizarre. I have never made such flowers myself, for I have neither the creative inclination nor the manual dexterity to do so. But I will give you a few ideas that I have either seen or read about to help you get started on this unusual craft, which is sometimes called altered flowers, contrived flowers, modified flowers, fun flowers, or even new-flowers-from-old.

The Chinese-lantern plant (*Physalis alkekengi*), with its attractively shaped, bright orange seedpods, is a most useful plant to have when making your own flowers. The closed pods can be used as the center of a flower or they can be cut carefully along the veins and opened to separate the individual "petals." If you want to open them even more to look like a petaled flower, the cutting and splitting of the pods should be done when they are not quite dry. The "petals" can be flattened out to expose the bright, shiny orange berry inside (Figure 36). If you are using wire to reinforce the stems, do not push it through the berries because it is so easy to loosen and damage them.

The round, silvery, paperlike inner parts of honesty pods (*Lunaria annua*), or the unrubbed seedpods, can both be used to make false

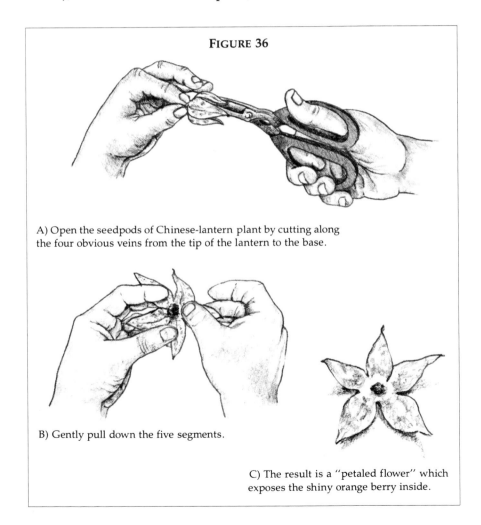

FIGURE 36

A) Open the seedpods of Chinese-lantern plant by cutting along the four obvious veins from the tip of the lantern to the base.

B) Gently pull down the five segments.

C) The result is a "petaled flower" which exposes the shiny orange berry inside.

petals. The center of the "flower" can be made with a strawflower bud (*Helichrysum bracteatum*), a tiny cone, or a calyx from Jerusalem sage (*Phlomis fruticosa*), to mention just a few possibilities. If, instead, you want the flower center to blend with the unrubbed purplish seedpods, use a seed head from love-in-a-mist (*Nigella damascena*).

Honesty pods can be tucked between the scales of cones, as can small leaves that have been preserved in glycerine (round *Eucalyptus* leaves are particularly suitable). Collect all shapes and sizes of cones, dry them (using Method 1 or 2), and use them to form the center of modified flowers. Dried maple seedpods can be used as the petals. The scales of cones can be trimmed to look like brown roses.

Another way to use honesty pods is to thread the stems through the tiny holes in the top of mature poppy seedpods, which are then secured with a spot of glue. You can either put many overlapping honesty pod "petals" to form a complex flower, or a few to form a more simple one. These holes around the poppy seedpod will only be present in fully mature pods when their color has turned beige. The immature pods can be dried (by Method 1 or 2) and are a very attractive gray-green color, but they will not have any holes. Grow a variety of poppy (*Papaver*) species in order to have a number of different sized seedpods to harvest and dry. You can choose from the huge Oriental poppies (*Papaver orientale*) that reach a height of 3 feet (90 cm), to the tiny alpine species (*P. alpinum*), which are often only 6 inches (15 cm) high.

Do you want to make your own Fugi or spider chrysanthemums? All you need are some mature poppy seed heads on their own stems and some glycerine-preserved pampas grass. *Small* pieces from a single head of the grass are glued into the little holes around the top of the poppy seed head. Be sure to make the flowers in a variety of sizes and also at different stages of maturity, from buds to fully open flowers. This can be done by varying the length of the pampas grass pieces and the angle at which they are inserted into the seed head (Figure 37).

The umbrella-like skeletons of members of the Umbelliferae family make good bases on which to attach petals or sepals (leaflike parts of the bracts) to make "flowers." Angelica (*Angelica archangelica*), dill (*Anethum graveolens*), fennel (*Foeniculum vulgare*), Queen-Anne's-lace (*Daucus carota*), and sweet Cicely (*Myrrhis odorata*) are some of the species from that botanical family. Others are listed on

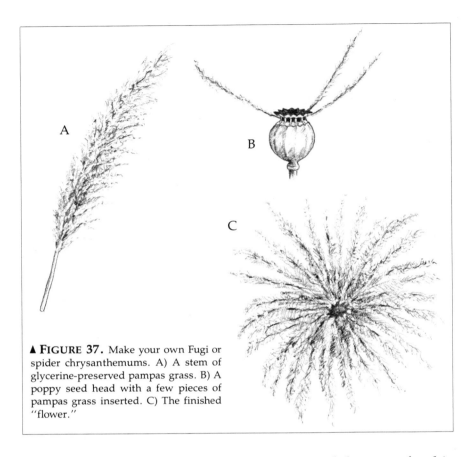

▲ **FIGURE 37.** Make your own Fugi or spider chrysanthemums. A) A stem of glycerine-preserved pampas grass. B) A poppy seed head with a few pieces of pampas grass inserted. C) The finished "flower."

pages 130 to 133, so hopefully you will save and dry some for this purpose.

To make a tuliplike flower, the pale green calyces of carnation, and other *Dianthus* species, can be dried in silica gel after the petals have been removed.

Lily-of-the-valley leaves that have been preserved in glycerine can be folded to form an Arum lily shape. They look attractive when wrapped around spiky dried material, such as hare's-tail grass (*Lagurus ovatus*) or squirreltail grass (*Hordeum jubatum*). Glycerine-preserved ivy leaves and the sheaths that enclose corn cobs can be used in this way. These sheaths can be preserved in glycerine either when young and green or when they are older and fading to a tan color (Method 15).

THINGS TO MAKE
WITH PRESSED FLOWERS
& LEAVES

THE HISTORY of pressing plant material goes back many centuries. Samuel Pepys, the seventeenth-century diarist, recorded a visit to the home of John Evelyn in 1665. He described Evelyn's winter (or dried) garden, saying that he "lays up leaves in a book" and by keeping them dry the color is preserved" and look very finely, better than any Herball."

There are dried flowers, still in good condition, at the Bodleian Library of Oxford University in Oxford, England, which have been there since the reigns of Charles I (1625 to 1644) and Charles II (1660 to 1668). They were collected in Virginia (U.S.A.) by a royal gardener and plant collector. These pressed plants were kept as botanical specimens, not for ornamental use. The best way for you to keep such specimens is in herbarium sheets.

Using pressed flowers, leaves, and unpressed seeds is not unlike doing embroidery, except that you are laying down the color and shapes with plant material instead of stitches. I have heard it called "painting with flowers," but I think the analogy to embroidery is more apt.

The many uses of pressed-plant material is a subject that requires a book all its own. I am only going to suggest some of the things you can make and briefly describe how to make them.

MAKING HERBARIUM SHEETS

Press the plant material you wish to preserve (method numbers and instructions are on pages 119 to 123 in Part II). Then when it is absolutely dry, lay it carefully under the protective plastic sheet of a "magnetic"-type photo album. Label it carefully with the name of the plant(s) and the drying date(s). Make notes in a diary as well—then you will have references for the future as to how long various specimens take to dry.

FRAMED FLOWER PICTURES

Obtain your frame first and then design the flower picture that will go into it. It is much more economical to use an old frame or to buy one at a thrift shop than to buy a custom-made frame to fit the finished picture. This may seem rather obvious, yet I do know people who have made a beautiful picture only to find that it would not fit in any standard-sized frame. If you have your heart set on an oval frame, be forewarned that they are hard to find and expensive if you do. Inexpensive round frames are not a problem because there are several sizes of embroidery frames available, but get one, if possible, without a tightening screw, which can be unsightly. If you can't find one without a tightening screw, cover the screw with ribbon.

After selecting a frame, choose your background. You can use drawing paper, construction paper, mat board, even blotting paper. Visit an art shop and see what is available. You can also use fabric. What type of fabric you use will depend on the type of picture you are designing, but coarsely woven linen, fine-weave canvas, velvet, cotton, or silk are just some of the materials that will complement different kinds of dried-plant material. Then decide if you want the picture to have a mat border that will lay over the background and picture.

Background material will have to be glued to a firm back board (plywood, heavy cardboard, etc.). Then the picture is "embroidered." Use stamp tweezers to pick up the plant material and a camel hair brush to smooth and arrange it. Then spot stick the pictorial elements with glue, allow the glue to dry completely, lay the glass on top of it, and assemble the frame. Nonglare glass is best because it will be lying directly on the flowers; regular glass could create unwanted reflections. You can, if you prefer not to use glue, reverse the procedure: lay out the plant material on the glass (already in the frame) and tightly secure the back board covered with background material into the frame.

► Grasses are attractive in the border as well as dried. Shown here are hare's-tail grass (lower left), ravenna grass (center), and other ornamental grasses.

▼ A colorful annual flower bed with plumed celosia in the center, statice in the foreground, and marigolds in the upper left.

▲ A border of acroclinium (*Helipterum roseum*).

◄ Globe amaranth (*Gomphrena globosa*).

► Honesty or money plant
(*Lunaria annua*).

▲ Chives (*Allium schoenoprasum*).

► Small globe thistle (*Echinops ritro*).

▼ Giant onion
(*Allium giganteum*).

185

◄ Cockscomb
(*Celosia cristata*).

► A dwarf zinnia cultivar (*Zinnia pumila, Zinnia acerosa*).

▼ Strawflowers (*Helichrysum bracteatum*).

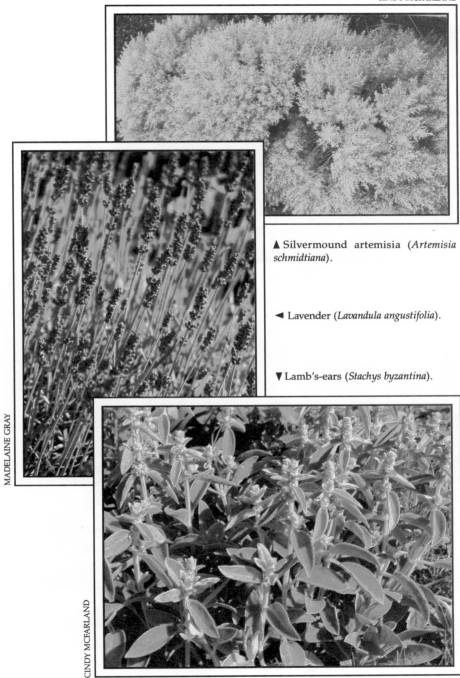

▲ Silvermound artemisia (*Artemisia schmidtiana*).

◀ Lavender (*Lavandula angustifolia*).

▼ Lamb's-ears (*Stachys byzantina*).

RICHARD W. BROWN

HUMPHREY SUTTON

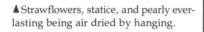
▲Strawflowers, statice, and pearly ever-lasting being air dried by hanging.

► A room well organized for drying flowers and plants. Hanging upside down are celosia, dahlias, delphinium, and strawflowers; flowers with short stems are air drying on a "shelf" of wire; zinnias and dahlias are drying in containers; and in the boxes are flowers being dried in a sand-desiccant combination.

188

▲ A wreath made with dried flowers and plants.

► A close-up of the wreath above that shows the featured flowers: strawflowers, statice, pearly everlasting, artemisia, sea lavender, and globe amaranth.

189

▲ Building a wreath on a framework of straw.

► A dried arrangement in a pottery container that includes baby's-breath, statice, and strawflowers.

UNFRAMED FLOWER PICTURES

If you don't want to frame your picture, you can cover it instead with plastic food wrap, but the back board and background material must be firm enough not to bend when the plastic is pulled tight. This plastic wrap should be secured on the underside with freezer tape. Remember that if you intend to use plastic food wrap, your picture must be at least 2 inches narrower than the width of the roll of plastic or you will not be able to pull it tight. With a tight seal, neither dust nor moisture will be able to damage your finished picture.

You can use semirigid, clear acrylic sheeting instead of glass or plastic wrap. This sheeting comes in several thicknesses and is sometimes used on sun porches and greenhouses. Affix the sheeting to your back board with plastic-coated cloth tape, which can be positioned so as to form a frame around the picture as well as seal it tight.

If you do not want to use glass, food wrap, or acrylic over your picture, you can spray it with an artificial sealant instead. But you should not use spray if your background is a delicate fabric, such as silk or linen, because the chemicals in some sprays might cause delicate fibers to deteriorate. Remember, a sprayed picture is much more susceptible to the elements and will not last like one that is airtight.

Small pictures displayed on an easel are not only attractive, but can easily be kept out of the sun. If you hang dried-plant pictures on a wall, be sure that the sun does not shine on that spot.

CARDS, TAGS, BOOKMARKERS, & CALENDARS

If your talents are more inclined toward miniature work, you can easily make your own greeting cards, bookmarkers, and calendars with dried-plant materials.

Greeting cards and hasty notes can either be covered with clear contact paper (available at craft, stationery, and hardware stores) or the pressed material can be stuck on the inside of the card (where you usually write the message) so that it is protected. Cards that need an envelope should be made to fit a standard-sized envelope. Gift tags, menu cards, and place cards do not need covering unless you want them to be lasting momentos. Bookmarkers look particularly attractive with a garland-type border; always cover them with clear contact paper. Large calendars can be made in the same way as unframed pictures (covered with plastic food wrap, acrylic sheeting, or spray sealant) and small ones like a large bookmarker.

PLACE MATS, COASTERS, TRAYS, & TABLES

To make place mats and coasters the pressed material is glued onto a piece of card stock that has first been backed with self-adhesive vinyl (the kind used to cover kitchen shelves). This is topped with a sheet of semirigid clear acrylic and the whole thing sealed and taped with self-sticking plastic-coated cloth tape (that could also serve as a border).

Trays can be made very attractive with a design of pressed flowers. They will need protection, but because glass cut to order is expensive and the end product heavy, it is better to make special mats to fit your trays in the same way you make place mats.

If you have a table topped with a sheet of glass, you have a wonderful "canvas" to work on. It will be a very big undertaking to decorate the entire tabletop, so get some practice on small projects first. Be sure you have enough pressed-plant material to complete the project before you start!

CARE & STORAGE
OF DRIED-PLANT MATERIAL

YOU HAVE GROWN, collected, and/or purchased flowers and leaves, which you have dried or preserved in glycerine. But if you do not want to use all of them immediately, they must be stored in such a way that they will retain their color and texture and will remain undamanged.

WHAT CAUSES DAMAGE

Dampness is the greatest enemy of dried-plant material. It can cause flowers to wilt and fade, and encourages the development of mildew. Whether your dried-plant material is being displayed or stored, an atmosphere that is air conditioned is the most preferred. A warm dry room is the next best thing.

To assure the quality of the atmosphere in your storage area, you can either keep a dehumidifier running or use a portable fan to maintain air circulation. If the climate in which you live is very humid you may need to provide a little warmth too, but if the climate is dry, neither a dehumidifier nor a fan may be necessary. Be sure that no plant material is placed or stored near any direct heat sources, such as heat registers, furnaces, fires, or electric baseboard heaters.

If possible, material that has been air dried by hanging should also be stored hanging; likewise if materials have been dried in an upright position they should be stored that way. But because this is not always possible, most air-dried material can be carefully stored, without damage, packed in boxes.

If you have used any kind of desiccant, plant material that has been dried in it needs more careful handling and storage than air-dried material. This applies particularly to material dried in silica gel because it becomes brittle and reabsorbs moisture very easily. To prevent this from happening, see pages 196 to 198 for information on storage and packing of desiccant-dried material. The thing to remember if you want flowers that were dried in silica gel to last when they are out of storage, is to keep them for projects that can be made airtight, such as those described on pages 199 to 201.

Glycerine-preserved plant material should not be exposed to dampness because mildew can form on the leaves if they "sweat." This material will not absorb moisture from the air, but if dried-plant material is stored nearby, it can easily be damaged by the moisture exuding from the glycerine-preserved material. Store glycerine-preserved plants in boxes, but not in plastic bags because of possible problems with the collection of moisture.

Sunlight must not be allowed to shine on *any* dried-plant material—it will become excessively brittle and the colors will fade. Keep it away from fluorescent lights too, which can cause color changes. All material in storage should be kept in darkness as much as possible.

Dust can spoil the appearance of dried plants. Use a photographer's blower brush on delicate material and canned air on sturdier stuff to blow dust off. If you don't have either of these tools, a feather and some patience does a good job on delicate material; a camel-hair brush will do the trick on heavier stuff. When material preserved with glycerine gets dusty it can be washed in warm soapy water and dried with a soft cloth.

Moths, weevils, and other bugs can damage stored material. Some people have suggested that mothballs be put in storage boxes to prevent insect infestations, but why risk your dried material smelling of them? Try storing a dried sweet-smelling herb that helps prevent insect damage, such as rosemary (*Rosmarinus officinalis*), lavender (*Lavandula* spp), one of the thymes (*Thymus* spp), or mints (*Mentha* spp) with your dried materials. Lavender cotton (*Santolina chamaecyparissus*), tansy (*Tanacetum vulgare*), common wormwood (*Artemisia absinthium*), and southernwood (*Artemisia abrotanum*) are all effective moth deterrents too.

Crowding dried-plant material in storage can do untold damage. Follow the recommendations given in the packing section that follows.

Packing Dried Material in Containers

Air-dried plant material can be stored successfully in cardboard boxes as long as care is taken when it is packed.

You will need shallow, fairly large boxes. Dress and suit boxes are a good depth, and the long boxes in which fresh flowers are shipped to florists are ideal for long-stemmed dried material. These florist boxes are often thrown away when they are unpacked, so they may be yours for the asking. When laying down dried-plant material for storage in a box, be sure to pack it in single layers.

Whatever material you are going to store in boxes, be sure it is in perfect condition: unwanted foliage removed, flower and seed heads intact, and, of course, no signs of mildew or rot. Bits and pieces that break or fall off can be saved for use in various projects. Store them in tins. Always put a sprinkle of silica gel in the bottom of the box, which you then cover with paper towels before packing it with the dried-plant material.

Tie delicate plant material into small loose bunches and wrap it in tissue paper and/or newspaper. Then lay the wrapped bunches alternately head to tail as shown in Figure 38. Stems with large flower or

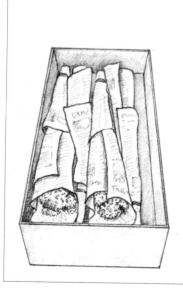

◄ **FIGURE 38.** To carefully store delicate air-dried materials, tie them into small loose bunches, wrap each bunch in tissue paper or newspaper, and lay them head to tail (without crowding) in a box or container.

seed heads can be laid singly in a box, as long as the heads are each supported by crumpled tissue paper. If the seed heads are *very* brittle it is better to hang them up individually.

Some material will not store well lying down. If you want to store it in boxes but keep it upright, choose a box that is taller than the dried plants. Then secure a piece of Styrofoam to the bottom of the box and push the stems of the material into it, spacing them carefully so that the plants do not touch each other. Or leave the material in the containers in which it was dried and put them in the box.

If the box has no lid, you can slip it into a plastic bag and close it with a twist tie. Don't forget to put a layer of silica gel in the bottom of the box and check every month or so to see if it needs reactivating.

Some people recommend putting holes in plastic bags when they are used for storage. If you are using silica gel in the bag, this shouldn't be necessary—it really depends on your climate and your storage conditions. You must also check inside the bags fairly frequently, especially during the first few months of storage, to be sure that no mildew has developed.

Individual flowers with short stems can be stored in a carton in which you have wedged a piece of plastic net canvas or rug-hooking canvas. The stems are then threaded through the holes. Be sure to put silica gel in the bottom of the carton and cover the top of the carton with plastic food wrap.

Glycerine-preserved plant material should be stored away from *all* dried-plant material—because it often exudes moisture, which could be reabsorbed by the dry material. I've said this before, but it *is* important to remember. Any visible moisture must be wiped off glycerine-preserved material or it will develop mildew. The atmosphere in which it should be stored needs to be neither too dry nor too warm, and though the material can be hung up, it is better to store it upright in tall cans or jars.

Any boxes used for storage must have air holes for ventilation and tissue paper should be laid down between the layers of plant material. Don't store it in plastic bags because without air it would sweat, develop mildew, and become damaged. *Never* put silica gel in any box containing glycerine-preserved plant material—it would be ruined.

Desiccant-dried plant material should be stored in a dark place in tins or plastic boxes that are airtight. Light cannot penetrate tins, but plastic boxes should be put inside an opaque container or dark cupboard. Always seal any box lid with freezer tape because it ensures a moisture-resistant seal.

When storing wire-stemmed flowers that have been dried face up, leave the wire stems bent at right angles to the flower heads (as it was while they were drying, see Figure 4); this will give them support in storage. Then put a little silica gel in the bottom of the container, cover it with a wad of tissues or cotton batting, place the flowers on the pad so that they do not touch each other, and cover it tightly.

Or dry some sand in the oven, cool it, and add a little silica gel as a dampness indicator. Put the sand about 2 inches (5 cm) deep in the bottom of the container, gently place your wired flowers on it, and seal it up. This is also the best way to store flowers with no stems. The sand will cushion the flowers and hold them upright, so that they retain their natural shape (Figure 39).

Whenever you use sand with silica gel as a moisture indicator, be sure to dry it out, or change it, if the silica gel changes color. If the sand gets damp, the dried flowers will reabsorb moisture and become useless.

To store flowers with short stems, put a piece of foam in the bottom of the container and push the stem into it. Put a little bag (nylon curtain material, 4 inches [10 cm] square, would be suitable) or silica gel in the container amongst the flowers, put on the lid, seal it with freezer tape, and label it with the date and what type of plants are therein.

▲FIGURE 39. To store dried flowers with no stems, put a layer of dried sand and a little silica gel in the bottom of a container, and put the flowers onto the sand without overlapping them.

It will be necessary to support flowers that have been dried face down so that the petals don't rest on the bottom of the container. Figure 40 illustrates how to do this, using the cardboard cylinders from rolls of paper towels. Put a little bag of silica gel in the box.

▲**FIGURE 40.** Flowers that have been dried face down will need to be supported in storage so that the petals won't be damaged. First, sprinkle a little silica gel on the bottom of the box and cover the silica gel with paper towels to prevent "burning." Using paper towel rolls, lay a roll at the end of the box, and rest the flower heads on top of it. Put the next roll down on top of the first wire stems, and repeat until there is no more space left in the box.

Pressed-plant material can be stored in a "magnetic"-type photo album, as recommended for herbarium specimens. Sometimes, when you are working on a project, you may find it more convenient to store pressed material in small stacked boxes. Space-saver, small-parts storage cabinets, such as handymen use to organize nuts, bolts, and nails, are practical and not expensive. Buy the add-a-drawer kind and you can expand the storage capacity when you need to. These small storage cabinets can be purchased at any good hardware store or from the catalog of a general merchandise retailer. Other storage suggestions include dental instrument cabinets or bird's egg display cases, but both might be difficult to acquire.

MAKING DRIED-PLANT MATERIAL
LAST FOREVER IN DISPLAY

SOME AIR-DRIED MATERIAL will last quite well in a reasonably dry atmosphere, but material that has been pressed or dried in a desiccant has a shorter "life expectancy." To guarantee that *any* dried-plant material will last for years in good condition, keep it airtight and free of dust.

WHAT TO USE FOR DISPLAY

Glass domes can sometimes be found in hobby and craft shops. If you are very lucky, you may find a genuine Victorian one in a second-hand or antique shop. They come in various sizes and usually have a wooden base on which the dome rests securely.

A glass- or plastic-covered cheese dish makes an excellent low-domed case. The base, whether it is made of wood, marble, or heavy plastic, will have a groove for the dome to sit in.

Glasses of all shapes and sizes, turned upside down, can be used as domes, but they should have a base. Wooden and glass coasters with raised edges and round glass ashtrays are obtainable in many sizes, so you should have no difficulty finding the right size base to fit the rim of any glass.

An aquarium can be used upside down on a wooden base, or you can use it right-side up. Have a piece of glass cut to fit the top of it.

Photo display cubes made of clear acrylic can be used to keep your plant material airtight and will display it beautifully. Make the arrangement on a block of oasis, secure it to the bottom of the cube with floral clay or glue, then slide the top in place.

Clear plastic spheres, available at hobby shops, are made so that the two halves fit snugly together and have a built-in loop from which to hang them. Or if you glue a plastic ring on the bottom to keep them from rolling, they can be placed on a flat surface.

Paperweights can be made using glass domes to cover pressed or preserved flowers that have been glued to a stiff fabric-covered base. Or kits that have comprehensive instructions for embedding plant material in liquid plastic can be purchased; it can be a complicated procedure, but the results are very rewarding.

Glass lamp chimneys (coal oil, hurricane) can be used if you make the arrangement sufficiently tall and narrow. Hurricane lamp chimneys are a better shape for arrangements and display than those of coal oil lamps. The tops must be covered with plastic food wrap (directions are on the opposite page).

Fish bowls can be used with food wrap as a cover.

Glasses right-way up can also be used with food wrap covers. Brandy snifters are particularly attractive.

Glass storage jars with covers make beautiful display cases. Look in secondhand and antique shops for old-fashioned candy-shop and apothecary jars. Some kitchen shops carry contemporary, but similar-shaped, containers. You can use the *lid* of an apothecary jar to hold a single bloom, which you would then finish in the same way as a paperweight.

Plastic storage jars with covers similar to the glass ones described above are another option.

HOW TO ARRANGE & SEAL DRIED PLANTS INSIDE DISPLAY PIECES

DOMES. If you are covering an arrangement with a dome, cut a cylinder-shaped piece of floral foam about 2 inches (5 cm) shorter and narrower than the inside of the dome itself. Then arrange your dried-plant material: pushing material with short stems into the foam, or gluing stemless material onto it. Then either stick the foam to the base with glue or secure it with floral clay and put the dome in place. The dome may or may not need to be secured to the base—it just depends on how snugly they fit together.

JARS WITH FITTED LIDS. If you have made an arrangement to display in a see-through container (rather than covering it with a dome) affix glue or floral clay to the bottom of the foam (a half-sphere shape is good for these arrangements). Make a "handle" to drop it in place by pushing a stick, pencil, or knitting needle a short way into the foam, then lower the foam onto the base of the container. If you use glue, let it set, then gently pull out the handle with a twisting motion; if you use floral clay, you can pull out the handle directly (Figure 41).

HOW TO MAKE AIRTIGHT FOOD WRAP TOPS. Put a few dots of white glue on the rim of a glass container and stretch the plastic food wrap tightly over it. Trim the plastic, leaving about a quarter of an inch (6 mm) overlap, which can be hidden with a band of ribbon glued in place and a bow, if you wish.

Before filling airtight containers with dried-plant material, be sure that the containers are absolutely dry. And once again, work in an area free of dust and dampness.

When filling airtight containers, secure the mechanics firmly and hide them with moss or carefully placed leaves.

HOW TO MAKE CHINA FLOWERS

Dried flowers can be sprayed with a clear-plastic oil-based resin, such as Varathane or Urathane, which will preserve them nicely and give them a sheen. You can also use a lacquer-based resin that will dry more quickly. Whichever you use (they can be purchased at a paint store), hold the can close to the flowers and give them a very light coat of spray. Allow the spray to dry completely between coats and repeat the procedure three or four times. The flowers, which will look as though they are made of delicate china, should last well, even in a humid atmosphere. It may be necessary, though, to spray them again occasionally to renew the luster.

FIGURE 41.

A) Starting the arrangement in a piece of foam.

B) Lowering the finished arrangement into the container by a knitting needle or crochet hook "handle."

C) The finished arrangement protected by its container.

First Aid for Dried- & Preserved-Plant Material

CLEANING. To clean air-dried plant material swish it gently in warm water. Change the water when it gets dirty and swish it some more. Dry it in the same way as it was originally preserved—that is, either by hanging it or standing it upright.

Glycerine-preserved leaves can be cleaned by wiping each leaf with a soft wet cloth and then drying it with a soft dry cloth. Or you can put a little cooking oil on a cloth, rub each leaf gently, then wipe each leaf again with a clean cloth to remove all traces of oil.

Desiccant-dried plant material should never be washed. Dust can sometimes be brushed off with a camel-hair brush, blown off with a photographer's blower brush, or if the material is sturdy, blown off with canned air. If the material is greasy or the colors dulled, throw it away—no amount of work can restore it to its previous glory.

STEAMING AIR-DRIED MATERIAL. If, in spite of your care, some flowers become crushed or flattened in storage, you can revive them by holding them in the steam of a boiling kettle. Then smooth the petals gently to restore their shape and form. Foliage treated with steam seldom needs to be touched up. In the steam the leaves will lose their creases and the stems will revert to their original shape. By putting a little pressure on steamed stems you can change their shape—giving them a new curve or taking out an old one. Such a task should be undertaken on a day when the humidity is low or your heat is on, so that the material will dry quickly.

GLUING. Desiccant-dried flowers tend to lose their petals more easily than flowers dried in other ways. To reattach them, apply a tiny spot of quick-drying clear glue to the base of the petal from a toothpick or small paintbrush. Support the petal for the few minutes it takes the glue to dry (Figure 42). Or while the flowers are still fresh, you can reinforce the petals at their base with a few spots of glue. Be sure to give the glue enough time to dry completely before putting them in the desiccant.

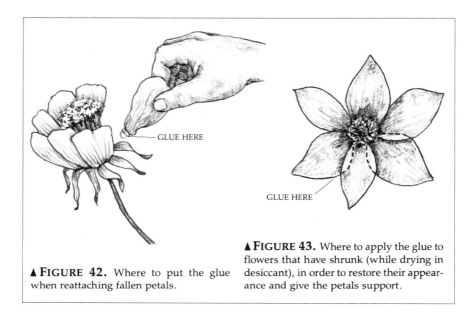

GLUE HERE

GLUE HERE

▲ FIGURE 42. Where to put the glue when reattaching fallen petals.

▲ FIGURE 43. Where to apply the glue to flowers that have shrunk (while drying in desiccant), in order to restore their appearance and give the petals support.

Sometimes single-petaled flowers shrink when drying in a desiccant so that petals which naturally overlapped no longer do and flop. To give them a little support, gently move the petals so that they overlap again and spot glue them together (Figure 43).

BLOWING. If the pods of Chinese-lantern plants (*Physalis alkekengi*) get squashed, make a tiny hole with a needle and blow into the pod. You can close the hole with a spot of glue.

SPRAYING. There seem to be several schools of thought about whether to use sprays or not. One extreme opinion would never recommend spraying, the other holds that one should spray everything! In practice, it is probably unnecessary to spray most air-dried material, although you may find that the seed heads of some grasses hold up better if they are sprayed. But pick, dry, and spray seed heads before they are mature.

If you are going to keep desiccant-dried (and especially silica-gel-dried) material in an atmosphere that is even slightly humid, then you will have to spray it so that it will "hold up." It is better to give the desiccant-dried flowers several very light coats of spray, but not so many that they become top heavy and lose their natural look. Glycerine-preserved material does not need to be sprayed.

MAKING A PROFIT
FROM DRIED-PLANT MATERIAL

THOSE WHO LOVE TO GARDEN or craft with dried-plant materials and have an entrepreneurial instinct, will discover a number of options open to them, some of which are described below.

- Grow flowers and leaves that can be dried or preserved and sell them fresh.
- Grow flowers and leaves, dry and/or preserve them yourself, and then sell them.
- Grow flowers and leaves, dry and/or preserve them, make arrangements, and sell them.
- Grow flowers and leaves, dry and/or preserve them, and make any of the projects described on pages 162 to 180 (unpressed plant material) and 181–82, 191–92 (pressed flowers and leaves).
- Grow some flowers and leaves and buy others, make arrangements or the projects described herein, and sell them.

৯ ৯ ৯

Let me give you a few examples of profitable cottage-industry-type businesses run by people I know.

One friend who has a big garden, grows and air dries flowers, selling some "as is" and making wreaths with others. Another grows a limited amount to dry in her small city garden, buys what she can't grow, teaches dried-flower crafts, and holds workshops as well. She also sells some items of her own making, having become well known through her workshops and teaching.

A friend in New Zealand cultivates over an acre of garden, grows flowers that air dry well, including many of the thirty-one plants in Part I of this book. She sells retail from her home on weekends, wholesales the dried plants to stores in her town, and has recently started doing some mail-order business. Another friend with some acreage also grows flowers that air dry well, and she grows garlic to make braids for sale along with the dried flowers.

Two other friends press wildflowers and flowers from their gardens. One makes exquisite pressed-flower pictures. The other specializes in the production of all kinds of original greeting cards that she sells to local gift shops and shops specializing in local crafts.

QUESTIONS TO ASK AND DECISIONS TO MAKE

- ❦ Are you a skilled craftsperson, and if you are, where do your skills lie?
- ❦ Should you specialize or should you make a variety of items for sale?
- ❦ Do you want to combine craft making with some growing and harvesting of plants? Or do you only want to grow and not do any craft work?
- ❦ Do you want to sell retail or wholesale or both?
- ❦ If retail, will you sell from your home, away from home, or both?
- ❦ If wholesale, how far from your home would you be willing to travel to make deliveries?
- ❦ Are you willing to sell on consignment, or would you rather give the retailer a larger discount (probably 40 to 50 percent of the retail price) and sell your products to him/her outright?
- ❦ Can you keep up production to supply a steady flow of good quality products? Whatever you do, don't make commitments that you cannot keep. Build confidence, and good business relationships, by being reliable.
- ❦ Do you want to sell all year-round or only during specific seasons such as Christmas?

POSSIBLE OUTLETS

If you sell retail from your home and/or garden, you must be there and available to customers at regular hours. You will find that, even though you state firmly that you are only open on the weekends, people will ring your doorbell every day of the week at any hour of the day! Be very sure that you don't mind losing your privacy before deciding to sell retail. It will also take up a lot of your time because retail customers usually like to chat as well as buy. However, you may prefer this to the more impersonal wholesale business venue.

You can sell retail away from home at farmers' markets and craft fairs, and display your crafts (if selling is not permitted) at agricultural and horticultural shows. Any of these places will also give you the opportunity to meet and learn from other craftspeople.

If you sell wholesale (which doesn't mean that you have to sell in large quantities, just that you are not selling direct to the consumer), there are many ways to market your products. Craft shops, gift shops florists, and bookstores may all be interested in craft items. For example, bookmarks custom-made for a bookshop are an obvious beginning, but the shop may be willing to take other items too. Specialty shops within department stores are another possibility. Don't bother to approach chain stores—they buy in multiple dozens or a gross (144)! Remember that it can become very monotonous to make a dozen or more of the same item, even though it was fun to make one or two. I am not, of course, referring to greeting cards or bookmarks, each of which can be quite different.

If you want to sell bunches of flowers, many of the outlets suggested for craft items could be approached. Is there a herb farm or a roadside produce stand near your home? Either of them might like you to grow and bunch everlasting flowers for them.

Is making floral arrangements your particular skill? The owners of linen and china shops, antique and gift shops who have display windows might consider an arrangement of dried-plant material to enhance the goods they have for sale. You could also cater to large furniture stores who have sample rooms on display. Restaurants and hotels are two more outlets for you to investigate. Don't forget banks, public buildings, and offices. You should be able to persuade them that dried flowers are more attractive than artificial ones. Start with your own doctor's or dentist's office!

ADVERTISING AND PUBLICITY

Except for small advertisements in local papers, you will find that extensive advertising is very expensive. An illustrated article about you and your work is more likely to generate interest and sales, so may exposure on a local television program. Go to craft fairs, and to any other shows where you can display your products, and do have an attractive business card.

You will find that consistently good quality products will bring you repeat orders, and that satisfied customers will send their friends and relatives to you.

WHATEVER YOU DECIDE TO DO YOU MUST

- ❦ Survey your markets thoroughly.
- ❦ Study the competition.
- ❦ Study craft and florist magazines for new ideas, but beware of making items that are too time consuming in relation to their commercial value.
- ❦ Try to produce some original items.
- ❦ Start small and expand as your business grows.
- ❦ Friends, particularly ones who grow everlastings, have told me that their biggest problem is keeping up with the demand—finding markets is no problem at all. Because they didn't want to take on paid help, some of them have had to cut out the more time-consuming products and specialize.

❧   ❧   ❧

The foregoing only offers general advice. It is difficult to be more specific without knowing where you live, how much garden space you have for growing, what your drying and storage conditions are, and what are your particular interests and skills. But you can't go wrong if you produce top-quality goods and maintain that quality. There is a big market and much enthusiasm for products that are hand-made with natural materials.

Perhaps the following quote will inspire you to great things. From the *New York Times*, September 1987: "LONDON—Since 1972, Kenneth Turner, florist to London society, and his young assistants have worked out of a richly scented London shop near New Bond Street that doubles as a showroom. Each year his efforts reach new heights of fantasy and price, which can be anything from US $3,000 to 'the sky' he said, for a big party. His products include dried-flower arrangements, huge baskets of roses and colorful mixed bouquets, expensive but long lasting. A $700 kitchen arrangement artfully combines wheat, artichokes, and baskets.''

So what are you waiting for? You'll never know what you can achieve until you try!

GLOSSARY

ANNUAL. *See* Hardy annual and Half-hardy annual.

AWN. The term most often used to identify the "beard" or bristly appendage often found on grains and grasses.

AXILS. The angle between a leaf or leaf stalk and the stem from which it is growing.

BASAL. The word used to describe the lower leaves of a plant, which can differ considerably from those on the stem.

BIENNIAL. Describes the life span of a plant that is sown one year and produces flowers and seed before it dies the following year.

BOLT. A plant is said to bolt when it produces seed prematurely, which can sometimes occur in very hot dry weather.

BRACT. A leaf or leaflike structure at the base of a flower stalk that encloses a flower bud. The so-called flowers of the poinsettia and the dogwood are actually bracts.

BUD. An unexpanded flower. Also used to denote an undeveloped stem or branch.

CALYX (plural is calyxes or calyces). The outer whorl, protective leaves, or sepals of a flower. Bells-of-Ireland (*Moluccella laevis*) and winter aconite (*Eranthis hyemalis*) have unusual and decorative calyxes.

COLD FRAME. A wooden or aluminum frame with removable glass or plastic covers, in which plants can be protected from inclement weather, and in which they can be "hardened off" before being planted in the garden.

COME TRUE. A plant is said to come true after propagation when it is an exact replica of its parent plant.

COROLLA. A collective name for the petals of a flower, whether they are separate or united.

COTYLEDONS. The primary leaves of an embryo plant, though the word is used for the first or "seed leaves," to distinguish them from the "true" or adult leaves. When the cotyledons are fully developed, and before the first "true" leaves appear, is the best time to prick out the seedlings, because roots are smaller and will be damaged less.

CUT BACK. To remove the growing tips and top parts of the stems, to encourage bushy plant growth. Also known as pinching back when done with the fingers. If done when the plants are older and woody, it is necessary to use secateurs.

DESICCANT. A substance that absorbs moisture.

FAMILY. Usually referred to as the botanical family or natural order (N.O.). A group of related genera (see Genus) with a family resemblance, but distinct from each other.

GENUS (plural is genera). A term used to indicate a group of plants that may be supposed to have a common ancestor and are similar in structure.

GERMINATION. The earliest stage in the development of a seed; its sprouting.

GRAFT. A graft is a union between two plants. Grafting is often used to propagate plants that are difficult or slow to raise from cuttings. It also can be used to propagate plants that do not come true from seed.

HABITAT. The natural and/or original home of a plant.

HALF-HARDY ANNUAL (H.H.A.). Cannot stand frost, and is usually started indoors. It is not planted out until all danger of frost is past. It will usually die with the first touch of frost in fall.

HALF-HARDY PERENNIAL (H.H.P.). Cannot stand frost, so is usually treated as a half-hardy annual. Or it can be dug up and potted before the first fall frost and put in a frost-free greenhouse or basement. It can be returned to the garden the following spring when there is no chance of any frost to damage it.

HARDEN OFF. The gradual exposing of plants, which have been raised under artificial conditions, to natural outdoor conditions.

HARDY ANNUAL (H.A.). A plant raised from seed, which flowers and dies within the year.

HARDY PERENNIAL (H.P.). Lives for at least two years and sometimes for as long as twenty. Some stay green all winter, others die back and reappear in spring.

HYBRID. The result of a cross between two parent plants that are dissimilar.

LATIN NAME. Or botanical name. Usually in two parts; the first is the genus, the second is the species.

LEGGY. A plant is said to be "leggy" when it has grown too tall too fast and thus becomes weak.

PETAL. One of the separate divisions of the corolla.

PINCH BACK. *See* Cut back.

POLYFILLA. A brand name for a cellulose filler used to repair plaster, wood, and wall board. It will not shrink as it dries and becomes so hard that it will take nails and screws. A good medium for sculpturing and modelling.

PRICK OUT. To transplant seedlings from the container in which they were originally sown to the flats or pots in which they will have more room to develop, prior to planting them out in the garden.

RAFFIA. Fibers from the leaves of a Madagascar or Brazilian palm tree. They are flat, soft, and smooth; and so do not cut into the stems of the plants around which they are tied.

RHIZOME. An underground stem or root stock in which some plants store nutrients enabling them to overwinter successfully.

ROOT STOCK. An underground part of some perennial plants from which new shoots and roots grow each season.

ROSETTE. An arrangement of petals or leaves in a roselike form. Seen in many alpines and succulents.

SCION. The term for any shoot or bud taken from one plant, and joined to another by grafting or budding, to form a composite plant. The scion provides the aerial shoots or branches.

SECATEURS. Pruning shears or clippers operated with one hand.

SEED. A ripened ovule that contains an embryonic plant.

SEEDBED. An area of soil worked to a fine tilth in which seeds are sown. After germination, the seedlings are thinned out and then later the plants are transplanted into their final beds.

SEEDLINGS. See Cotyledons.

SEEDPOD. Usually any pod or capsule containing seed(s), though technically it is a dry fruit that splits open.

SPECIES. A group of individual plants all belonging to the same genus.

THINNING OUT. The removal of excessive seedlings which have appeared because the seed was too thickly sown. Should be done as early as possible in the plant's life, to avoid disturbing the roots of the plants which are to remain. It can be done in two stages, e.g., if the plants are to stand 8 inches (20 cm) apart, the first thinning out should leave a plant every 4 inches (10 cm). Later, as they begin to touch, a final thinning can be done.

SOURCES OF SEEDS AND PLANTS

The businesses listed below are specialists and include many everlasting flowers and plants among their specialties. All of them give both the common and the Latin name in their catalogs and on their packets of seeds, which indicates that they know exactly what they are offering and you know exactly what you are ordering.

Goodwin Creek Gardens
Jim & Dotti Becker, Proprietors
P.O. Box 83
Williams, Oregon 97544
U.S.A.
(503) 846-7357

This is a family owned and operated business. They are organic growers of over 250 varieties of herbs and everlastings, selling plants and seeds through the mail (seeds only to Canada). They have many varieties and colors of hard-to-find everlastings. They also sell everlasting notecards, handcrafted wreaths, and other items made with dried-plant material. Send .50¢ for their catalog.

Richters
Goodwood, Ontario LOC 1A0
CANADA
(416) 640-6677

They sell seeds and plants, shipping to the United States as well as Canada. Send $2.50 for their catalog. It is full of useful information as well as listing seeds of everlastings, alpines, and herbs (including some that are suitable for drying for decoration). Many of the seeds listed are difficult to find elsewhere. They also sell vegetable seeds for the gourmet, potpourri items, wildflower seeds, posters, books, gardening supplies, and more. They sell both retail and wholesale at the nursery, by mail, and by alternate parcel services.

Suffolk Herbs
John & Caroline Stevens
Sawyers Farm, Little Conyard
Sudbury, Suffolk C010 ONY
ENGLAND
Bures (0787) 227247

An interesting and comprehensive catalog. They have an excellent listing of seeds for growing plant material for drying, including the True Everlasting flowers, Perpetuelles, seeds for plants that produce thistlelike heads or seedpods, and ornamental grasses and grain seeds. They also list many herb seeds and plants and cottage garden flower seeds, which include many that can be dried for decoration, as well as seeds of many hard-to-find vegetables.

The addresses of three big seed houses follow. They carry a wider variety of garden flowers than the specialists listed above. Occasionally you will find some everlastings listed in such catalogs in a group by themselves, but I have often found these lists to be incomplete. Many other everlastings can be found in the general list of flower seeds—you just have to take more care when reading the catalog in order to find them.

G. W. Park Seed Co., Inc.
Greenwood, South Carolina 29646
U.S.A.
(803) 223-7333

A very comprehensive catalog of flower and vegetable seeds.

Thompson and Morgan, Inc.
P.O. Box 100
Farmingdale, New Jersey 47727
U.S.A.
(201) 929-0028

The U.S. address of this well-known British seed house.

W. J. Unwin, Seedsmen
Histon, Cambridge CB4 4LE
ENGLAND

Offering an excellent listing of vegetable and flower seeds, including many everlastings.

For further information about sources of supplies, consult the classified ads in craft magazines, such as *Crafts 'n' Things*, and the Yellow Pages in your telephone directory.

BIBLIOGRAPHY

Amlick, Barbara H. *Getting Started in Dried Flower Craft*. New York: Bruce, 1971. Toronto & London: Collier Macmillan. Basic instructions for gathering, drying, pressing, and arranging dried-plant material.

Bolton, Eleanor Reed. *Dried Flowers With a Fresh Look*. New York: D. Van Nostrand, 1958. Unusual, practical, and informative.

Carico, Nita Cox, and Jane Calvert Guynn. *The Dried Flower Book: A Guide to Methods and Arrangements*. New York: Doubleday, 1962. Good, step-by-step instructions.

Cramblit, Joella, and Jo Ann Loebel. *Flowers are for Keeping*. New York: Julian Messner, div. of Simon & Schuster, 1979. An excellent, how-to craft book for children.

Darbyshire, Jane, and Renee Burgess. *Dried and Pressed Flowers*. New York: Arco Publishing, Inc., 1984. London: Collingridge. Section on pressed flowers is very comprehensive and well illustrated. Useful information in dried flower section as well.

Floyd, Harriet. *Plant it Now, Dry it Later*. New York: McGraw-Hill, Inc., 1973. Unusual and interesting; there is a section on recreating famous flower paintings.

Foster, Laura Louise. *Keeping the Flowers You Pick*. New York: Crowell, 1970. Toronto: Fitzhenry & Whiteside. The author is a distinguished botanical artist and her black-and-white illustrations are exquisite.

Foster, Maureen. *The Art of Preserved Flower Arranging*. London: Collins, 1984. Practical how-to line drawings and excellent color photographs of arrangements.

Gordon, Leslie, and Jean Lorimer. *The Complete Guide to Drying and Preserving Flowers*. Secaucus, N.J.: Chartwell Books, Inc., 1982. Exeter, U.K.: Webb & Bower. Mostly about pressed flower crafts; has delicate illustrations. There is small, and good, section on how to use unpressed materials.

Hillier, Malcolm, and Colin Hamilton. *The Book of Dried Flowers: A Complete Guide to Growing and Arranging*. New York: Simon & Schuster, Inc., 1986. London: Dorling Kindersley. Magnificent color photographs, but it has more on arranging than growing.

MacDermot, Elizabeth. *The Art of Preserving Flowers*. Toronto: James Lewis & Samuel, 1973. Useful lists of plants.

Mierhof, Annette, and Vlamings. *The Dried Flower Book: Growing, Picking, Drying, Arranging*. New York: E. P. Dutton, Inc., 1984. Practical and well illustrated with delicate flower paintings.

Morrison, Winifrede. *Drying and Preserving Flowers*. London: Batsford, 1973. Practical and well illustrated.

Ohrbach, Barbara. *The Scented Room.* New York: Clarkson N. Potter, Inc., 1986. An original idea with exquisite color photographs.

Shipman, Dorothy, and Moyna McWilliam. *Everlasting Flower Craft.* New York: Arco Publishing, Inc., 1975. Newton Abbot, Devonshire, U.K.: David & Charles. A practical craft book, well illustrated, with line drawings and black-and-white photographs.

Squires, Mable. *The Art of Drying Plants and Flowers.* New York: Bonanza Books, 1958. Good period and contemporary designs.

Stevenson, Violet. *Dried Flowers for Decoration.* London: Collingridge, 1955. Newton Abbot, Devonshire, U.K.: David & Charles, 1972. A comprehensive and practical book.

Taylor, Jean. *Plants and Flowers for Lasting Decoration.* London: Batsford, 1981. Good sections on using dried and pressed flowers for decorating. Well illustrated.

Thompson, Dorothea. *Creative Decorations with Dried Flowers.* New York: Hearthside Press, 1965. Practical how-to drawings and photographs.

Vance, Georgia S. *The Decorative Art of Dried Flower Arrangement.* New York: Doubleday, 1972. The various styles of flower arrangement throughout history are well described; also has practical how-to information.

Subject Index

Numbers in **boldface** indicate drawings or photographs appear on that page.

Plant Name Index